P. -50

GW00675108

Motoring on Regional Byways
DEVON AND CORNWALL

CHRISTOPHER TRENT

Motoring on Regional Byways

DEVON
AND CORNWALL

G. T. FOULIS & CO. LTD.
HENLEY-ON-THAMES · OXFORDSHIRE

First impression May 1969

© Rupert Crew Ltd 1969

SBN 85429 094 **X**

MADE AND PRINTED IN GREAT BRITAIN BY
MORRISON AND GIBB LIMITED, LONDON AND EDINBURGH

CONTENTS

ILLUSTRATIONS

BYWAYS OF DEVON AND CORNWALL

DEVON AND CORNWALL have won world-wide fame as a holiday paradise, to which hundreds of thousands come every year to enjoy the sea at the many resorts along the beautiful coastline. One of the principal reasons for the popularity of the two counties is that together they form a peninsula jutting out into the Atlantic and are thus blessed with a long coastline broken up into the wide bays and tiny coves beloved by holidaymakers. Small wonder that the people of Devon and Cornwall are proud of their heritage and that the many who come from other parts of the country to settle there soon absorb the strong traditions.

The coastal scenery of both counties needs no underlining, from the rugged slate rocks of north Devon and Cornwall to the colourful red sandstone and white chalk of south Devon's cliffs. The picturesque fishing villages which grew up round every sheltered cove where it was possible to build a harbour have become the favourite resorts of today.

Inland the great granite masses of Dartmoor and Bodmin Moor, distinguished by their characteristic outcrops of rock known as tors, were centres of prehistoric culture, a wonderful hunting ground for the archaeologist. Over the whole area links with prehistoric man are found, from the groups of hut circles to the burial chambers and stone circles.

The Romans left few traces of their occupation west of Exeter, the terminus of the great Foss Way which ran across England from Lincoln, though there were Roman roads to the west of this point and there is evidence that Cornish tin was mined by the native people under the Romans. The occasional stone with a Latin inscription also suggests at least temporary occupation, probably by legionary forces.

There is a rich legacy, however, from early Celtic times in the many stone crosses, often beautifully carved but generally of primitive workmanship. The ruins of only two Celtic oratories, believed to date from the seventh century, exist in north Cornwall but the dedication of so many of the churches to Celtic saints leads to the conclusion that a number were built on the site of early chapels. The extraordinary number of surviving Norman fonts, many with elaborate and intriguing carving, is further evidence of the early foundation of churches which now show little sign of their ancient history.

These churches are often handsome, whether in the warm red sandstone or in the sombre grey granite, the majority ennobled by tall battlemented towers with graceful pinnacles. The exquisite wood carving found in nearly every church, at its most splendid in the rood screens and bench ends, is testimony to the artistry of the medieval craftsmen; fortunately most of these carvings escaped the wave of destruction that followed the spread of Puritanism.

The historic towns, and the lesser market towns too, are treasure houses of mellow buildings dating from medieval times onwards, while many beautiful manor-houses and noble mansions, some of them open to visitors, are linked with families celebrated for their distinguished ancestors, especially, as would be expected from counties with seafaring traditions, the great sailors, past and present, such as Drake and Raleigh.

In exploring the river valleys of Devon and Cornwall, famous for their lovely wooded banks, we shall find villages as delightful as those by the sea, especially the groups of thatched cobb cottages round a green typical of Devon. Mawgan-in-Pydar is an outstanding example of the inland Cornish village.

The fine pasture land of Devon valleys and the fertile red soil of the south produce two of Devon's best-known products, Devonshire cream and cider. Cornish cream is equally celebrated, and pottery made from local clay is found everywhere. Even the signs of industry add a picturesque touch to the rural scene, from the ruined chimneys and buildings of the old tin workings to the weird landscapes formed by the vast pyramids of china clay waste.

For the motorist Devon and Cornwall offer almost unlimited scope, for in addition to the main roads there are literally thousands of miles of minor roads to be explored by the adventurous tourist, taking him to places where even in the height of summer he will meet few other cars. It is probably true that it is difficult to find a beach or cove that has not been 'discovered' by the many, but even this is possible, especially out of the peak season. Only on Dartmoor are the roads across the high moor few and far between, and here it is worth driving over those which have necessarily become main roads.

In the cultivated country, however, little roads connect farm with village, and village with local market town, and even those that were only tracks until comparatively recent times are now surfaced. Cliff tracks have also been surfaced in many places, so that miles of cliff road can be enjoyed from which there are splendid sea and coastal panoramas. The typical ferny-banked lanes mostly remain narrow, as they always have been, and mean slow going but the scenery to which they give access is ample reward for patience.

A word of warning on this subject. Some of the roads near the popular seaside resorts, and the quaint old streets in the fishing villages, are narrow and bound to be congested in the main holiday months. It is, of course, much easier to see these places out of the season, when it is possible to drive round the streets. Otherwise it is only practicable to explore them on foot, which in any case is well worth doing if we are to get any impression of the charm and atmosphere which bring so many people back year after year to Devon and Cornwall.

CHAPTER TWO

THE ENGLISH RIVIERA

MENTION THE NAME 'TORQUAY' to almost anyone in this country and to many millions abroad, and the words 'English Riviera' will immediately spring to their minds. It lies in a perfect sheltered position on Torbay, its white houses scattered among the wooded hill which rises from the harbour giving a continental appearance, which the semi-tropical plants in the lovely gardens reinforce. Because of its mild climate it has been a favourite Devon watering-place since the beginning of the nineteenth century, and this popularity has extended to Paignton, Brixham and the resorts of Babbacombe Bay.

In spite of the fact that most of Torquay dates only from the nineteenth century, including most of its churches, its links with the past go right back to prehistoric man, for Kent's Cavern, which lies off the Babbacombe road near Ilsham church, was occupied as early as the Old Stone Age, reoccupied in Romano-British times, and yet again in medieval times, evidence of all these inhabitations having been revealed by patient excavation. In historic times, Torre Abbey was founded near the end of the twelfth century as a Premonstratensian monastery, and there are considerable survivals from the original buildings, including the gatehouse and the tithe barn. The later Georgian mansion on the site now houses the town's art gallery.

The mother church of Torquay, St Saviour's at Tor Mohun east of the abbey, retains much of its medieval work, including the tower, and has some interesting early monuments.

Paignton and Brixham are old towns, each with a medieval church, and Paignton has the fourteenth-century Kirkham House and the grandiose Oldway House open to visitors. The old fishing village of Brixham achieved fame as the landing place of William of Orange in 1688, commemorated by his statue beside the harbour. Its little museum is fascinating for those interested in the history of an ancient fishing community.

4

The 'picture-postcard' village of Cockington lies within the boundaries of Torquay, and here again the church is a medieval one, originally Norman, with a good fifteenth-century screen, and the village itself consists of an outstanding group of thatched cottages and the famous blacksmith's forge. The beautiful gardens of the sixteenth-century Cockington Court are open for visitors to wander beside the lovely lakes and along the flower-lined paths, and refresh themselves at the Court.

It is superfluous to add that the accommodation of Torbay and the resorts in the vicinity is almost inexhaustible and is able to serve the varying needs of every kind of holiday-maker.

Torbay is the key to the wonderful scenery of the coast and the inland expanses of Dartmoor. The tours in this chapter, and the following one devoted to Dartmoor, are all routed from Torquay and the surrounding towns, but can, of course, be followed from any place on the route by joining in at the appropriate place and following the tour back to that point.

Tour one: Dartmouth, Totnes

The first tour takes us across the Dart to the historic town of Dartmouth and to the other ancient town upstream, Totnes, as well as many other smaller places on and near its banks, and covers approximately sixty miles.

We leave Torquay along the sea front to Paignton (A379) and there follow the road signs for Dartmouth, noticing on the right as we leave the town a huge exotic popularly known as the Big Tree. Where the road forks after several miles take the right branch to the higher ferry. It is worth while making an early start in the busy season, as the queues for the ferry can be considerable at times. Dropping down to harbour level we have our first sight of the Dart estuary and as we cross it we have a closer view of the many craft belonging to the Royal Naval College, the Edwardian buildings of which are the dominant feature of the opposite slope as we approach Dartmouth.

The ancient port of Dartmouth is full of historic interest and needs half a day spent there to see even the principal features. Its position on a natural harbour just above the mouth of the Dart made it an ideal point of assembly for fleets setting out on warlike missions, as well as for peaceful commerce. Originally the village was centred at high-set Townstall, where the fourteenth-

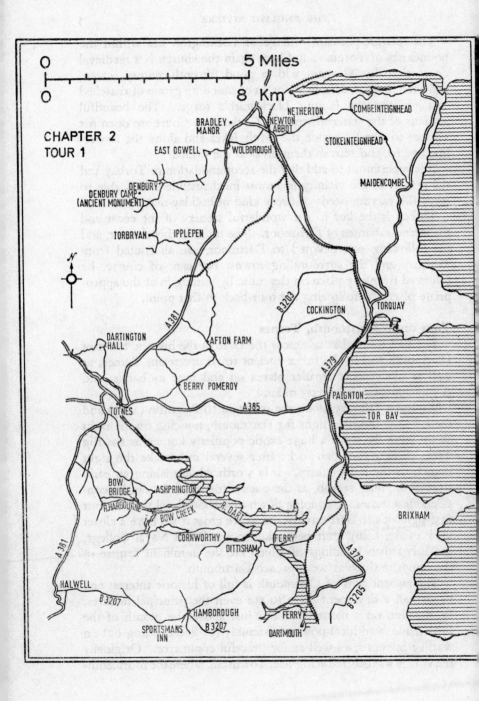

century parish church of St Clement still stands. However, towards the end of the same century the accent had shifted to the growing settlement near the harbour and the Church of St Saviour was dedicated in 1372. This church was constantly enlarged and embellished until it became the magnificent building which has come down to the present day. Its glory is the elaborate fifteenth-century rood screen and here, unusually, the rood stairs at each end still exist. The contemporary pulpit is of carved and painted stone, with the badges of King Charles II added in painted wood. The striking altar with carved and painted figures of the four Evangelists was formerly a late Elizabethan communion table. Add to these the spacious gallery carrying the arms of seventeenth-century mayors and other notables, two good brasses, the old south door dated 1631 (now inside the church) with ironwork showing two stylized lions under a spreading tree, and the early fire-engine formerly kept in the porch ready for emergencies, and it becomes clear that the church has much to show.

The castle, in a strategic position downstream from the town and facing its opposite number at Kingswear, was first built soon after the completion of St Saviour's church and only a few fragments of this early work have survived. The present structure (open to the public daily) was built in the fifteenth century, with later additions, much of it in a good state of preservation.

In addition to these medieval links with Dartmouth's past there are many fine houses in the town, including the row of merchants' houses known as the Butter Walk. One of these is used as the town museum, while an upper room above the chemist's shop has a unique plaster-work ceiling showing the Tree of Jesse. Two other especially interesting houses are in Higher Street, reached by a stepped path off the road to Bayard's Cove (where there is a small sixteenth-century fort and a stone commemorating the visit of the *Mayflower* on its way to America). One is the Cherub House, recognized by the attractive carved figure of a cherub on the corner, a timber and plaster building dated 1380, and the other, sometimes known as Shambles House, is a three-storeyed gabled Elizabethan building. Finally, a little museum houses the first steam engine of Thomas Newcomen (1663–1729), the 'Father of the Steam Engine', who was born and lived in Dartmouth.

We leave Dartmouth continuing on the A379, passing the Butter Walk, then, on the right in Victoria Road, the market place and one-storey market house. The road climbs steeply through Townstall, giving a retrospective bird's-eye view of the town and harbour. At the summit we fork right and join B3207 and after about two and a half miles we turn sharp right at the Sportsman's inn for Dittisham, i.e. take the nearest of the two roads forking off, and in Dittisham village turn right for the passenger ferry. The village has some pleasant old houses but its fame rests on the plum orchards in which it is set and which produce the excellent Dittisham plums. There is a delightful corner at the ferry, with parking space for several cars on the beach and grand vistas up and down stream and across the estuary to the wooded slopes of a low hill, to the left of which is Galmpton Creek.

Returning to the junction at the top of the village street, turn right for Cornworthy, passing close to the Perpendicular church, and a steep narrow lane brings us in about half a mile to the head of a creek of the Dart. Bear right at a pond and as we continue to Cornworthy between fern-clad banks we reach a high view-point where there is a lay-by for those wishing to pause for a longer look at the scene. We drive through Cornworthy past the church and as we leave the village we pass on our left the Gothic gatehouse and fragment of the chapel of a priory of Augustinian nuns. At this point turn right for Totnes, and at the next junction go on for Ashprington, passing Tuckenhay paper mill and soon reaching Bow Creek. At the Waterman's Arms at Bow cross the Harbourne river by an old stone bridge then turn right, again for Ashprington, and soon reach this village of stone houses of pleasing appearance. At the war memorial cross turn left for Totnes and as we ascend we have several good views through farm gates on our left. We eventually join the Kingsbridge road (A381) into Totnes, which gives a clear view of the impressive Norman motte and bailey castle, approached by a turning to the right. The castle is open daily (afternoons only on Sundays) to visitors on payment of a small fee and, apart from its historic interest, gives an unrivalled view down the Dart valley from its highest rampart.

To see the town park on the Plains near the river at the foot of Fore Street and walk up the main street past the museum and under the fifteenth-century East Gate, noting the many gabled

The river Dart at Totnes. (Chapter 2.)

The July Fair at Kingsbridge. (Chapter 2.)

Dartmoor ponies.   (Chapter 3.)

The Dart at Hexworthy bridge.   (Chapter 3.)

Elizabethan houses with overhanging upper storeys and the Butter Walk supported by granite pillars, as at Dartmouth. From the East Gate the line of the old town walls can be followed, and the old guildhall stands beside the church, the latter enhanced by the tall red sandstone tower and containing many features of interest, particularly the splendid stone screen.

From Totnes make a detour by the A384 to visit the scene of one of the most successful educational experiments of modern times, the Trust founded in the 1920's by Mr and Mrs Elmhirst of America, which is centred on the beautiful medieval mansion of Dartington Hall and now expanded into a complex of school buildings which include indoor and open-air theatres. There are farms, woodcraft and other rural craft centres among the many enterprises. Visitors are allowed to walk round the grounds, which are at their best in late spring during the flowering season of the trees, underneath which a woodland carpet of cyclamen and other spring flowers delights the eye. (Car parks are provided.)

To reach Dartington follow the Exeter road (A384) beyond Shinner's Bridge and turn right by the church, a landmark with its tall tower and crown of elaborate pinnacles. The road through the grounds takes us past the hall in a roughly semi-circular direction until we rejoin the outward road near Totnes and turn right into the town to resume our route. This time we leave by the Paignton road (A385), which crosses the Dart, after a mile bearing left for Berry Pomeroy by a slate-hung former toll house. There it is worth turning aside to see the church, which has some imposing monuments of the Pomeroy and Seymour families, before proceeding to the castle they built, which is open to visitors on payment of a small fee. The original castle was built by Ralph de Pomeroy, a friend of William the Conqueror, and enlarged in later centuries. The ruins of this castle remain side by side with the later mansion built by the Seymours after the Lord Protector had acquired the castle and manors in the reign of King Edward VI.

We continue past the castle and at a junction go forward on the Newton Abbot road. This plunges down to cross a tiny brook and on the ascent we turn right by Afton Farm into an unsign-posted lane. This little road takes us over a crossroads, under a railway bridge, and across the main Newton Abbot road, directly into Ipplepen. On reaching the village we make for the church, guided by its tall pinnacled tower, there going on for Torbryan, a mile away. Here we must drive off the road for a few yards to see the church, entered through an old lych gate. It has a fine screen and contemporary pulpit. Nearby is the Church House inn, which is dated 1400. On regaining our road we follow the signposts to Denbury, lying under a low hill crowned by the entrenchments of an Iron Age camp which gives the village its name. In the centre we turn right by the square stone lock-up for East Ogwell, which is reliably signposted, there turning right, then left (signposted Newton Abbot), and with the church to our left go forward uphill, bearing left at a u-junction and left once more at a subsequent junction, the signpost reading Newton Abbot in each case. This soon brings us to the main road, where we turn left towards the town, on its outskirts passing on the left the entrance to Bradley Manor, a typical fifteenth-century stone manor-house open to the public on Wednesday afternoons from April to September.

If we are not visiting the manor-house on this occasion and have previously seen Newton Abbot, we can avoid the drive through the busy town centre by crossing the main road where the road from East Ogwell joins it, and driving through Wolborough, passing its solitary church well away from the village, and rejoining the main road at the other end of the town.

Newton Abbot is an ancient market town which has had a Wednesday market for over seven hundred years, though it has greatly extended its boundaries and consists of Newton Bushel and the parishes of Wolborough and Highweek on the hillsides above. William of Orange was proclaimed King in the market place after his landing at Brixham in 1688. Only the tower of the old church of St Leonard remains as a landmark at the central crossroads, and we take the right-hand lane for Torquay as we approach it, turning immediately left along East Street, continuing on the Torquay road until we come to the junction with B3195, where we turn left towards Teignmouth. This takes us over Milber Down to Netherton and Combeinteignhead, where we turn right at the post office for Stokeinteignhead, a village with some charming thatched cottages near the church, where there is the oldest screen in Devon, dating from the reign of King Richard II, and many quaint figures carved on the capitals of the nave piers. From there we continue to Maidencombe, turning right for Torquay at the main road.

Tour two: Dartmouth, Start Point, Kingsbridge

The next tour, of about seventy-five miles, takes us farther afield along the fine stretch of coast beyond Dartmouth to Start Point and touches the most southerly point of Devon, coming back through the old market town of Kingsbridge.

From Torbay we drive to Dartmouth, as for the previous route, but this time we fork left on the road for the Lower Ferry (B3205). This road takes us down an enclosed valley, hence does not give

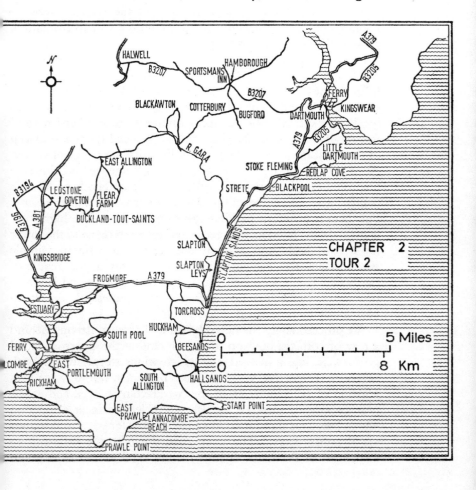

us the splendid views afforded by the road to the Higher Ferry, but as we drop down through woods to water level we have an incomparable panorama of Dartmouth and the Royal Naval College across the harbour.   After the car ferry has been nudged across by tug to the Dartmouth landing stage turn right, then take a steep left hairpin bend for Dartmouth Castle, rising steeply out of the town, later seeing Kingswear Castle on the other side of the harbour.   At the castle turn we keep straight on uphill then turn left at the first crossroads for Little Dartmouth, obtaining from the single-track road grand sea views towards Start Point and rounding the head of a combe leading down to Redlap Cove.   We join the main road, the A379, on the outskirts of Stoke Fleming and drive through the village on the way to Blackpool, passing the church on our right.

From this point we have a series of wonderful coastal views which can only be seen from the main road, so we must follow it for the next few miles.   First we look down to the lovely sandy bay of Blackpool, its beauty enhanced by the fine trees surrounding it.   Luxuriant fuchsias and hydrangeas are another beautiful feature of this part of the ride.   As we descend the whole sweep of the coastline as far as Start Point lies within our line of vision. After passing through the small village of Strete we look down to Slapton Leys, lagoons enclosed by the raised beach of Slapton Sands.   Part of the beach has been designated a nature reserve but there is generous parking space on the rest.   The higher ley is now almost filled in with reeds and between this and the lower ley a road leads into Slapton village, just beyond the simple granite memorial 'presented by the U.S. Army to the people of the South Hams who generously left their homes and lands to provide a battle practice area for the successful assault in Normandy in June 1944'.

We proceed along the raised beach to Torcross, driving behind a row of cottages built on the beach, and at the Torcross Hotel go forward into a hedged lane which winds steeply uphill, with several retrospective views to Start Bay.   On our way we pass a group of tall pine trees of the Mediterranean type and at the next crossroads turn left for Beesands, left again at a junction where Beeson is signposted, then follow the signposts to Beesands via Beeson village.   The steep road down to the little fishing settlement of Beesands, famous for crab and lobster fishing and

the making of lobster pots, ends near the inn, so we must return
to the first junction. There we continue forward uphill, at the
top going forward again for Huckham.   At a junction by an old
stone house turn left, descending into a combe which reaches the
sea at North Hallsands, and left at a fork beyond a group of farm
buildings, left again at a T-junction and, a short distance farther,
right uphill past a row of pretty cottages.

On reaching a wider road turn left for South Hallsands and
Start Point, continuing towards the latter until we reach the
entrance to the Devon Trust Nature Reserve, where there is a
car park and a perfect spot for a picnic.   To see the lighthouse we
follow the coast path on foot.   We must retrace our way to the
first junction and turn left for South Allington, later neglecting a
track which turns off to Lannacombe beach, then turning left
where South Allington is again signposted.   This narrow road
takes us first through woods and in half a mile to the village,
where we turn left at South Allington House for Prawle, then
left again in less than half a mile for East Prawle.

East Prawle is the most southerly village in Devon, only a mile
as the crow flies from Prawle Point, the most southerly point.
Unfortunately we are not crows and the nearest we can get to
Prawle Point by car is a rough turning place beyond the coastguards station, reached by the 'No Through Road' which leads
from the green in the centre of the village, though there are
footpaths to the point and along the coast.

From the green we drive past the post office, and at a farm at
the end of the village turn left (away from Kingsbridge), turning
left at the next T-junction for East Portlemouth.   We leave the
Portlemouth road for a turning to Rickham which gives access
to the National Trust Rickham Common and brings us to
Portlemouth church, dedicated to St Winwaloe.   As we drive
down towards the shore we are looking down to the Salcombe
and Kingsbridge estuary.   We leave the ferry road on our left
(passenger only) and take the tidal road round the estuary to
South Pool, rounding the head of several creeks.   After crossing
a ford we have to negotiate a steep ascent with a difficult
left-handed hairpin bend but otherwise the road is passable.
Eventually we reach South Pool at the head of a long creek,
which we round by crossing a stone bridge into the pretty village
and turning left immediately along the other side of the creek,

which is also crossed by a ford and stepping stones. Often white
ducks swimming in the stream that runs into the creek complete
the peaceful scene.

We soon leave the shore of the creek and drive over hilly
country for about two miles, first turning right and later left at a
T-junction. This brings us to Frogmore at the head of Frogmore
Creek, where we turn left into the village, the older part of which
lies on the main road, A379. Continue on this road to Kingsbridge, and after passing through the Charletons follow the road
down to the Kingsbridge creek, crossing an arm of the creek by
an arched stone bridge. There is a large car park at the head of
Kingsbridge creek for those who wish to explore the town on
foot, and also for those who are attracted by cruises on the
estuary as far as Salcombe.

There are many interesting old buildings in the steep Fore
Street, which leads up from the creek, among which are the
Shambles, with a covered walk supported by granite pillars of
1585, next to the guildhall surmounted by an unusual clock.
During the period of the traditional July Fair a stuffed glove
decorated with a posy is hung outside the shambles, which used
to indicate that no one would be arrested while the fair lasted,
but it is not wise to count on this dispensation at the present day!
The spired church dates back to Norman times, though little
Norman work survives, and the old grammar school, founded in
1670, is just beyond the Georgian Methodist Chapel.

We leave the town at the top of Fore Street by B3196 and at the
next main crossroads turn right on the Halwell road (B3194), then
right for Ledstone, crossing a main road, the A381, on the way
to the village. We turn left at a junction as we wind through the
village, and after a steep climb turn left then immediately right
at a staggered crossroads. In less than half a mile we come to the
pretty centre of Goveton and there turn right for Buckland-Tout-
Saints, represented only by the solitary Georgian Gothic church.
Descend alongside a park planted with exotic trees and past the
estate lodge into a deep valley, densely wooded on the farther
side, then by a pretty slate-hung house beside a stream turn left.
The road is steep, and muddy in places at times, but improves
beyond the entrance to Flear farm and it takes us straight to
East Allington in about a mile and a half. In the village we go
forward past the church, right at the Fortescue Arms, and right

again at the post office, where Blackawton is signposted, towards
which we continue over the next three crossroads (the last one
unsignposted). In another half mile cross Bow Bridge over the
Gara river, which flows into Higher Slapton Ley, and take the
Cotterbury road uphill through a hamlet. At the crossroads by
Cotterbury Forge we go forward with the forge on our left along
the road to Bugford. There it is straight forward at the signpost
then turn left in a few yards for Hemborough and reach a major
road in three-quarters of a mile. We turn left and continue on
this road all the way to Halwell, a distance of about three and a
half miles over pleasant green landscapes with a steep hill at the
end which is prohibited to heavy vehicles. We turn right on A381
at Halwell church, dwarfed by its massive tower, which brings
us back to Totnes in little over five miles, and thence back to
Torbay.

Tour three: Teign valley

The last tour in this chapter, covering about seventy miles,
explores the beautiful Teign valley and the countryside to the
north of Torbay as far as Exeter. From Torquay clock tower
leave via the town centre and A380 for Newton Abbot, or from
Paignton left at the Grand Hotel past Torquay station, and left
again for Torre station. Both roads join at Torre station, where
we take St Michael's Road almost opposite the station, i.e. we
turn right just before the station if from Torquay, or cross the
main road if from Paignton. At the top of the hill turn left in
Barton Road and continue through Barton, crossing a small
roundabout in about a mile where motorists from Babbacombe
can join the tour via B3198, turning right on reaching the roundabout. At the top of Barton Hill Road take a left fork for
Daccombe, soon descending through woods, and on the descent
bear right, again for Daccombe. Before we reach Daccombe the
woods give way to quiet farming landscapes and low hills.

At a pretty group of thatched cottages in Daccombe (one a few
yards along the road to the left bears the date 1468) we go
forward for Stokeinteignhead and at a subsequent unsignposted
fork bear left up a single-track lane with high hedges which in a
short half mile brings us to a wider road. Care is needed as we
turn right into it, as this can be a busy road at times. We follow
this road until it joins the main coastal road at Maidencombe,

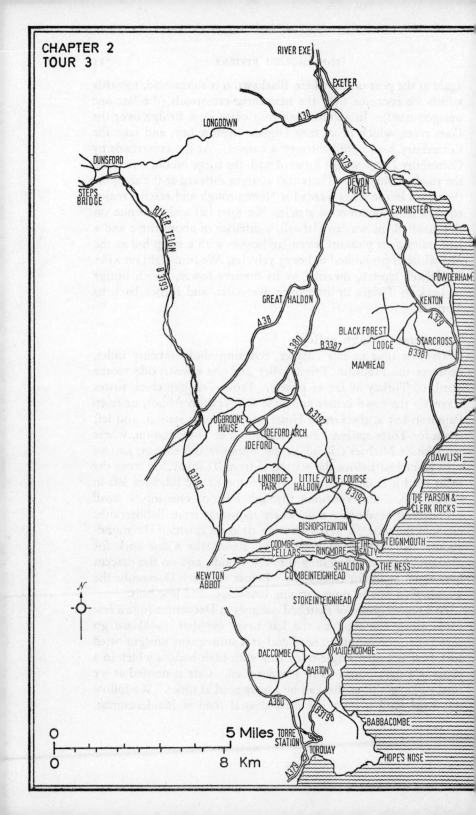

turning left into the latter for a brief stretch until a road leaves it on the left for Stokeinteignhead. The way is now straight-forward to Stokeinteignhead, where we continue to Combe-inteignhead, there turning right for Shaldon and Teignmouth to drive closely beside the estuary, enjoying the views across the wide expanse. At Coombe Cellars there is a large waterside car park, but only for patrons of the inn. However, a short distance farther there is a lovely cove where there is parking space for several cars. Before we reach Shaldon we pass the red sandstone Ringmore Towers, its massive battlemented square structure strangely out of keeping with its surroundings.

In Shaldon we turn left by the seventeenth-century Hunter's Lodge to cross the bridge into Teignmouth but the way into the village centre is straight ahead past the lodge, and beyond it a road beside the strand with colour-washed houses leads to The Ness. Shaldon's central green and many pretty corners with thatched cottages make this detour worth while. Teignmouth is an important port and 'fashionable watering-place' since Regency times. Miraculously the waterside town has remained unspoilt through the two centuries and is as popular as ever as a holiday resort, with plentiful accommodation. Many attractive Regency houses survive, the *pièce de résistance* being Den Crescent behind the grassy Den, the colonnaded Assembly Rooms flanked by contemporary Regency houses in a harmonious composition. The vistas are magnificent wherever we look: from the Den promenade east to the remarkable Parson and Clerk rocks, beyond the red cliffs to the white chalk ones of east Devon, and on a clear day to the conical Golden Cap on the Dorset coast; across The Salty to Shaldon anchorage, almost invariably dotted with gay pleasure craft, and The Ness, crowned by trees planted to mark Queen Victoria's jubilee, and beyond it to Hope's Nose; from the bridge to Teignmouth harbour and up river towards Dartmoor.

The churches of East and West Teignmouth are its main links with the Middle Ages but both have been rebuilt in the nineteenth century, St Michael's, near the beach, in a mixture of Norman and Gothic styles, St James's more adventurously in an octagon shape, contrasting curiously with the plain red sandstone tower of the original church.

We leave the town by B3192 for the steady climb to Haldon

Moor, which attains a height of 827 ft, our view to the left extending across Coombe valley to the southern slopes of Dartmoor. A road from Dawlish comes in on our right, a convenient point for Dawlish motorists to join the tour via Haldon Moors road, which starts from the parish church at the back of the town. The golf course on our left is the highest point of Little Haldon and thereafter on the right we look over Dawlish and Exmouth as far as the Dorset coast, and even beyond the yellow sandstone of the Golden Cap as far as Portland Bill on days of exceptional visibility.

We descend gently from Little Haldon before starting the climb to Great Haldon, its dense woodlands contrasting with the State Forest's orderly dark conifers broken up by the necessary wide fire-breaks, and enlivened by the bright yellow gorse and purple heather in the flowering season. On reaching A380 we turn right towards Exeter, driving under mature beech trees, with beautiful hanging woods on the escarpment to our right. After three-quarters of a mile we turn right, then leave the main road in under half a mile for a lesser road (B3381) on the right, signposted Starcross, Dawlish and Mamhead, which takes us through dense woods to Black Forest Lodge. This is a fine shelf road, giving splendid views over the Exe estuary and left to Exeter, and winds steeply downhill, so that it is advisable to drive slowly in order to enjoy the scenery as well as for safety's sake.

A quarter of a mile beyond the crossroads at Black Forest Lodge, where the way is forward, turn left for Kenton, and this minor road brings us into the village opposite the church, which many motorists miss when driving through on the main road. This is a pity, for the Church of All Saints is an exceptionally good fourteenth-century building in red sandstone with a noble tower and is claimed to be a perfect example of the West Country Perpendicular style. The fifteenth-century rood screen is outstanding in a county of beautiful screens, richly carved and painted, with forty panels of saints and prophets at the foot, and the contemporary pulpit was lovingly restored under the aegis of the Rev. S. Baring-Gould from fragments found in a school cupboard! Interesting details are the heads of King Henry IV and his Queen, Joan of Navarre, on each side of the south porch entrance, and a second representation of Henry IV on the column to the right of the tower arch. On the triangular village green beside the main road is an ancient Celtic cross, a link with an early church which was on the site of the present one and was possibly dedicated to St Petrock, who is thought to have founded it or visited it in 560.

From the church we retrace our way on the Mamhead road and in less than a quarter of a mile fork left through a cutting in the red sandstone and continue in this single-track lane for a mile and a half to a T-junction with a major road (B3381), where we turn left. At the next T-junction Starcross is signposted and we drive through the village, turning left along A379, then leave the main road in less than half a mile for the turning to the right for Powderham, thereafter looking across the Exe to Lympstone and Exmouth. The deer park of Powderham is on our left and through the trees we have an occasional sight of the castle, which is open daily in the afternoon during the summer months (except Saturdays). This fine medieval castle, still a family home with period furniture and portraits of the seventeenth to the nineteenth centuries, was built in 1390 by Sir Philip Courtenay, ancestor of the present Earl of Devon. On this route we pass the exit from the castle, so when visiting it we must stay on A379 from Starcross as far as the main entrance.

The road turns inland at Powderham church, which is reputed to be connected with the river by underground passages formerly used by smugglers. Inside the church there are several monuments to the Courtenays and an early stone tomb with an effigy believed to be Elizabeth de Bohun (died 1316), daughter of Edward I and mother-in-law of the Third Earl of Devon. After leaving the church we shortly pass the exit from the castle near a group of thatched cottages and in just under a mile and a half cross A379 into a single-track road which brings us in little over a mile to Exminster. There we rejoin A379, a left turn needing care, and within half a mile turn sharp left beside a school along Deepway Lane, in about threequarters of a mile forking right, soon after this junction obtaining a grand view through pine trees (where there is a lay-by) to Great Haldon, surmounted by Belvedere. We see Exeter ahead and soon reach the Exeter by-pass beside the Devon Motel. Here we cross the by-pass into the Alphington road (A379) and thence follow the signposts into Exeter, crossing Exe Bridge to see the city if we have not previously visited it (see page 37).

We leave Exeter by Exe Bridge and A30, so that if we are not going into the city on this occasion we merely turn left on A30 without crossing the bridge. Within two miles of the centre we leave A30 for the Moretonhampstead road (B3212). Keep to this road for several miles, forking left, still on the B3212, at the war memorial cross in Longdown. The road follows a high ridge with rolling farmland and deep combes on either side. We come down to the Teign valley at Steps Bridge, where the river leaves its gorge on the way from its source on north Dartmoor. The wild daffodils on the river banks by the bridge are a sight not to be missed in early spring, but not to be picked, for this flower was in danger of disappearing and is now protected.

From Steps Bridge return for about a quarter of a mile then take the first turning to the left (currently unsignposted) just short of a red-brick chapel. This little road brings us to Dunsford, into which we turn right at a T-junction. The village has many attractive houses strung along the main street and a grey stone church in the Perpendicular style. At its end we proceed towards Exeter and turn right at a T-junction beyond a group of pretty cottages by a tributary stream of the Teign. When we rejoin B3212 we turn right, then leave it at the next junction, turning left on B3193. This pleasant road runs closely beside the river Teign, crossing it in under half a mile by an old stone bridge and heading through the well-wooded valley. Frequently we are close beside the river, its banks lined by many graceful trees, and our way is marred in only one place by a vast quarry and works.

On reaching A38 we turn left in it to cross the river and railway, leaving it again immediately afterwards for a lesser road just beyond the riverside road. This is a steep tree-shaded road from which we have one of the best distant views of Chudleigh Rocks over a stile on our left. Turn left at a T-junction along a road bounded by an estate wall on the right and a descending wooded escarpment on the left and at the next T-junction turn right for Ugbrooke and Teignmouth. This road after leaving the park of Ugbrooke House leads to Ideford and after going under the motor road we shortly also go under the old brick Ideford Arch, soon entering the village. At its end we turn right at the T-junction for Bishopsteignton, passing one entrance to Lindridge Park, open to visitors in the summer season, and later the imposing main entrance with wrought-iron gates is on our right as we turn left towards Bishopsteignton. At the next crossroads, however, we turn left for Haldon to bring us back to the golf course, where at the triangular junction (around which the heather is especially luxuriant) we go forward for Teignmouth but after a few yards turn right along an obscure gravelly track which is signposted 'public footpath'. This leads to a parking space 800 ft above sea level, one of the finest viewpoints across the Teign estuary to The Ness and Shaldon, most striking towards sunset, and of the hinterland reaching from the coast to Dartmoor.

When we reluctantly turn away from this memorable panorama we continue as far as the golf house and beside the entrance turn right and drive steeply downhill all the way into Teignmouth (low gear is necessary for much of the way). In the built-up area we go straight on (Dawlish motorists here bearing left to return via the coast road) and at the main road T-junction turn right, then almost immediately left to cross the bridge over the Teign to Shaldon and so back by the coast road to Torquay and Paignton.

CHAPTER THREE

DARTMOOR

DARTMOOR is a word with many connotations and though known to all conjures up in their minds many different pictures. To some it represents an area of menacing tors and bogs, to others a perfect place for a walking and climbing holiday, a mecca to the geologist, naturalist and archaeologist, and, less happily, a firing range for the army, and a prison originally founded for prisoners of war when England was threatened by Napoleon. Nevertheless it is safe to assume that the moor is known and loved by Devonians and that it is visited by all who spend holidays in the county.

Even the most barren part of the moorland has an appeal and fascination of its own, and the many prehistoric sites are interesting to the layman as well as to the expert. On our travels we shall notice the low dry-stone walls, the recently afforested areas, the green river valleys, and the less frequent fields. We shall hope to see some of the hardy Dartmoor ponies (and please do not feed them; there really are good reasons for not doing so), and in addition to the traditional breeds of Dartmoor sheep and cattle there are Scottish black-faced sheep and Galloway belted cattle with their distinctive white bands, while buzzards are often seen swooping overhead.

In the following tours we shall visit the famous highlights of scenic beauty and many less well known but often equally lovely places. They are routed from Torbay and neighbouring towns, but can easily be joined from the many popular resorts of the moor itself, e.g. Chagford, Moretonhampstead, and Bovey Tracey, which all have good accommodation, and through which the tour passes.

Tour one: Fernworthy, Chagford, South Tawton

The first tour covers just under 100 miles from Torbay back to Torbay and visits many of the villages and small towns on the eastern edge of the moor as well as penetrating as far as the roads

will allow towards its heart. From Torquay we drive to Newton
Abbot on A380 and continue on the same road as far as Kings-
teignton. (Motorists from Teignmouth and Dawlish can join the
tour by driving to this point via A379 and A381, turning right
into A380 for a few yards.) Just beyond the junction of A380
with A381 turn left along a quiet country road and soon after
passing a ball clay works on the right turn left again to cross the
river Teign, the Stover canal and the railway in quick succession,

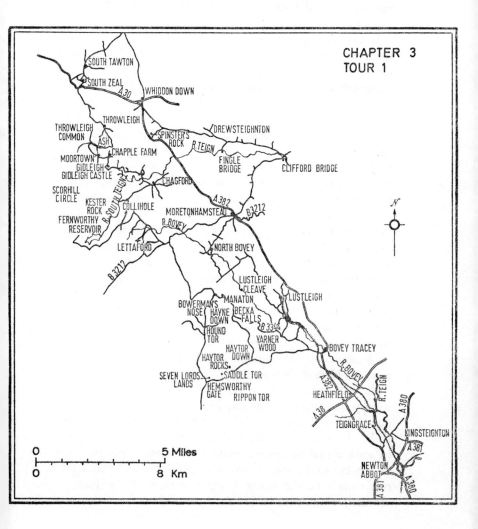

finally crossing a long causeway over the marshy water meadows before turning right for Teigngrace.

In the straggling village, which has a late Georgian church containing monuments of the Templer family of adjoining Stover Park, there is a mighty oak with a split trunk. A short distance beyond Teigngrace we cross a stream, then turn left for Bovey Tracey along a straight road for over two miles through woods and heathland, crossing A38 at Heathfield, a ball clay manufacturing centre, and turning right into the main road (A382) which leads to the town on the other side of the Bovey river.

Bovey Tracey is a deservedly popular centre, rising on a slope from the river with the church at its highest point. The first church on the site is believed to have been built as a penance by one of the knights who murdered Thomas à Becket in 1170, and certainly the dedication is St Thomas of Canterbury. The present Perpendicular church has a splendid screen, on which is represented scenes thought to represent the quarrel between King Henry II and Becket. Other interesting features are the stone pulpit with coloured figures and motifs, the fifteenth-century brass lectern, and the two chancel monuments with life-sized effigies, while the royal arms at the west end are those of King Charles II.

To resume our way recross the river and turn right between the Dartmoor and Dolphin hotels, in two hundred yards going over a level crossing and in half a mile bearing right at a fork for Manaton and Becka Falls. Along this pleasant road the hedgerows are enlivened by many holly trees, glowing brightly in the sunshine in a good berry season. Beside the next signpost for Becka Falls the attractive Dartmoor pony emblem informs us that we are entering Dartmoor National Park. On the left the vast Yarner Wood nature reserve, where a woodland trail which may be followed by the public has been established, stretches out towards Haytor Down.

Beyond the wood we emerge on the open moor, climbing steeply towards the summit, but at first with wooded vistas to our right, and after a mile we re-enter woods as we near Becka Falls. Here there is a car park and we must take the opportunity to walk down to see the massive boulders marking the course of the Becka Brook, which is scarcely visible even after heavy rain, much of the water being diverted by the leat (artificial channel) which runs beside the road. There is a refreshment hut

Beer Head. (Chapter 4.)

Chiselcombe bridge, river Lyn. (Chapter 5.)

Ilfracombe, the harbour. (Chapter 5.)

Cotehele, houses near the Tamar. (Chapter 6.)

at the foot of the steps for those who wish to pause for sustenance before the return climb.

From here continue for only a short distance, turning sharply left into a single-track lane signposted Leighon. We cross a ford —often dry—and beyond it a tiny stone bridge before beginning the steep climb to the open moor through a natural woodland of ancient moss- and lichen-covered trees among thick undergrowth and ferns. Emerging from the woods, we are soon well above the 1,000-ft contour on a shelf road giving retrospective views towards Manaton and to the rock-strewn slopes of Lustleigh Cleave on the left (cleave means a steep slope). Later we are looking down into the Bovey Basin, a vast dried-out lake with deposits and fossils of a prehistoric sub-tropical age where the ball clay is now obtained.

A cottage on the left in a dip as we round a sharp bend marks the western limit of Yarner Wood and we subsequently follow the lower slopes of Haytor Down until we see the massive granite outcrop of Haytor Rocks (1,491 ft). We turn right into a major road at Long Barn café, passing the Moorland Hotel, and as we drive close beside Haytor Rocks can see the quarry from which was obtained the granite for London Bridge, now in America. Two spacious car parks suitable for picnicking are on our left at the nearest point to the rocks.

Our road thence takes us past the appropriately named Saddle Tor (right) and Rippon Tor (left). Red flags flying indicate that firing is taking place on an unhappily sited firing range. However, we proceed over miles of bracken-covered moor, relieved by the bright green roadside verges and clumps of heather and gorse, especially in autumn.

The next junction is at Hemsworthy Gate, where, the map tells us, we are driving beside Seven Lords Lands, one of the many intriguing names found on Dartmoor. Here bear right for Widecombe but leave the Widecombe road half a mile farther, taking the right fork for Hound Tor, soon seen silhouetted on the skyline. We avoid a lesser road on the left which leads to Bell Tor, Chinkwell Tor and Honeybag Tor, and soon Hound Tor reappears ahead before the road dips gently and for a time is tree-lined, the beech trees on the left growing on top of a stone wall. The road rises high again to pass near the foot of Hound Tor, the slopes below which are bluebell-covered in spring and where there is a parking space. At a junction beyond the tor take the middle of three roads, our way signposted Bowerman's Nose. This road goes through farm land and there may be a gate to open at each end. Bowerman's Nose is on the slopes of Hayne Down on our right in about a mile from the junction, a curious rock formation standing apart from the rock mass on the summit.

On leaving the open moor our way is through a narrow tree-lined lane to a T-junction with a wider road, the B3344, where we turn left for Moretonhampstead, left again at the next junction, signposted Widecombe, then right again for Moretonhampstead at a post box. Now we continue on this road, going forward at a junction by a farm where our way is signposted Chagford, and arrive at the junction with B3212, where there is an ancient wayside cross. Turn left towards Princetown at this point but in a quarter of a mile turn right into a minor road for Lettaford, then go forward for Fernworthy, descending to cross the infant Bovey.

After this take the third turning on the left for a detour to the lovely Fernworthy reservoir in its forestry setting, a sharp bend which is more easily negotiated by using the parking space on the other side of the road in turning. We proceed, undeterred, along the way marked 'No Through Road' and soon enjoy unrestricted views to an immense Forestry Commission plantation and later our first sight of the reservoir, which lies at a height of almost 1,200 ft in the upper valley of the South Teign which, with its tributary streams, feeds the lake, in fine weather a beautiful sapphire blue enhanced by its dark green setting. Enter the plantation through a gateway, driving above the lake beside larches, though the lake is still visible through the trees, later looking across to the plantations on the farther shore. We cross the several streams feeding the reservoir as we round the head and at the end of the surfaced road there is a parking space, suitable for picnics, near one of the loveliest lake scenes. Although the vast plantation extends for over a mile to the reservoir and for over two miles from north to south, it is tastefully laid out and cannot be said to spoil the appearance of Dartmoor, as many critics declare has been the case in other areas.

As we return to our route the views are different and just as beautiful and when we come into the open we can see as far as Exmoor on a day of good visibility. We retrace our way only as far as the first junction, there bearing left for Collihole and

Kestor Rock. The latter is seen at several points along the next few miles, recognizable as a massive block against the skyline. At the next junction we turn right for Chagford in sight of a cluster of buildings high on our left and in half a mile reach the outskirts of Chagford.

Chagford has through the ages been an important market town on the edge of Dartmoor above the valley of the Teign, one of the four Stannary (from the Latin word for 'tin') towns created by King Edward I. The Stannary courts acted as a kind of separate parliament (nominally under the Crown) to enforce the strict laws and to deal with all matters arising in connexion with the tin industry. The Chagford court operated until 1790. The town has a typical Dartmoor granite church with a tall tower and a restored market cross on granite piers in the centre, the polygonal sides carrying tiny shops. The Three Crowns inn, formerly the home of the Whiddon family, is an interesting stone house with mullioned windows and a handsome two-storeyed porch.

From the market place return to the first fork by the Moorlands Hotel, there taking the right branch, and in just over a quarter of a mile cross a three-arched medieval bridge over the Teign. The road from this point is steep and winding for about half a mile before passing through a hamlet and descending through woods beside a brook, which we later cross and ascend to Gidleigh village. At a green triangle where Throwleigh is signposted turn right into the tiny village centre, consisting chiefly of the towered church and the remains of a small Norman castle beside it. The castle may be visited daily (afternoons only on Sundays) on payment of a small fee, and the mainly thirteenth-century ruined keep has two storeys and a cellar in a fair state of preservation.

A few yards beyond the castle turn right for Throwleigh but soon leave this road for a turning on the left beside the farm buildings of Chapple Farm. Where Moortown is signposted we go forward and soon regain the open moor, turning right for Ash at a junction beyond a stream, the course of which we follow, later turning left away from it by some farm buildings, and in less than a quarter of a mile left for Throwleigh at a little triangular green with a solitary horse chestnut. We pass the inn of this hamlet in a few yards, then bear left at a later fork, half a mile beyond which is the centre of Throwleigh. Turning left at the cross erected to commemorate Queen Victoria's Diamond Jubilee in 1897, on the base of the fifteenth-century village cross, we pass the exceptionally lovely group of church and fifteenth-century church house attached to the lych gate, here again turning left and winding uphill to Throwleigh Common, where we turn right at the T-junction.

We are now on the edge of an area of Dartmoor where the links with prehistoric inhabitation of the moor are more than usually numerous, many of which can be seen from the motor roads, others only reached on foot, e.g. the fine Scorhill stone circle. Our road is heading for the northern edge of the moor in the direction of Okehampton, the smooth oval dome of Cosdon rising on our left to nearly 1,800 ft, an example of a rounded granite hill. The many stone monuments and hut circles on its slopes are evidence that it was densely populated in prehistoric times. We follow the foot of Cosdon for nearly two miles after leaving Throwleigh Common, our road signposted South Zeal and Okehampton, and on approaching a major road we fork left under the road bridge to reach South Zeal, turning left in the village to ascend the pleasant main street. We first pass on our left the Oxenham Arms, formerly a mansion of the Burgoyne family, noting the imposing two-storeyed porch and Tudor coach entrance, higher up the street the small chapel with its quaint pinnacled bell-cote, and at its west end the old village cross on high steps.

Near the top of the village, at a crossroads beyond a thatched inn, turn right for South Tawton and immediately see the upper stage of its tall church tower ahead. There is the stump of a wayside cross on the right at the junction before we reach the centre, where we shall find an outstanding composition even for a county of lovely villages. Surrounding the ancient 'Cross Tree', a village elm surmounting a granite plinth, are the church and church house attached to the lych gate, and nearby the inn and a number of charming thatched cottages. The two-storeyed church house with external stone staircases and Perpendicular east window is Elizabethan, while interesting features of the church are the pretentious John Wyke monument and the polished wooden pulpit beautifully inlaid with figures of saints and foliage, resembling a piece of early Georgian furniture rather than an ecclesiastical work.

We drive a few yards beyond the church and turn right where

a large yew tree stands outside one of the thatched cottages. After passing an ancient cross, this time complete with its head, (in about a mile and a quarter) we go forward at the ensuing signpost towards Spreyton, which is also signposted at the next junction. When we arrive at a T-junction we turn right for Whiddon Down, there crossing A30 and almost immediately turning left at a fork to a second main road, A382. An extensive view of the moor with Cosdon is seen briefly as we turn left in the main road and leave it at once for a left turning, Drewsteignton being signposted at both points. The signposts are thereafter reliable over the three miles to Drewsteignton. After a mile a signpost on the right shows the way to the prehistoric Spinster's Rock, a famous megalithic tomb with a huge capstone balanced on three upright stones. It stands in a field near Shilstone farmhouse.

Drewsteignton is another attractive village with many thatched cottages around and near its spacious square. At one side is the high-set church and churchyard commanding extensive views, and on another the Drewe Arms, outside which is a horse's head tethering post beside the inn sign. We leave by the road signposted Fingle Bridge, retracing our way for a few yards from the church to the junction. The road to the bridge is steep and narrow and needs caution but at its end there is a parking space and a café by the medieval bridge, and on the other side there are tracks for walkers. At this point the Teign is in the steepest part of its magnificent wooded gorge.

Returning to the signposted junction, go forward for Dunsford and in just under two miles descend steeply into the gorge again. At the crossroads turn right for Moretonhampstead and cross the river by Clifford Bridge, passing the attractive Clifford Farm, then climb steeply out of the gorge to a high viewpoint looking north over the plantations towards Exmoor. Thereafter the way is straightforward to Moretonhampstead, where we turn right at the library, immediately left, right at the pleasant Georgian White Hart, then left along Pound Street for North Bovey, and continue on the North Bovey road. Before we leave Moretonhampstead we should drive towards the church, turning into Cross Street to see the almshouses, an interesting seventeenth-century building with an arcade of round arches and granite columns. Near them is the base of the village cross, now crowned by an elm tree, while the head of the original cross lies beneath it.

The way is direct to North Bovey, with only one crossroad before we reach the outskirts of this delightful village of beautiful thatched and whitewashed cottages set round a spacious green dotted with mature oak trees, among which stand the old village cross and pump. Keeping the green on our left, we pass the picturesque post office and then the church, dipping down to cross the river Bovey by a long stone bridge and causeway. In three-quarters of a mile turn sharp left, continuing for about one and a quarter miles, recrossing the Bovey within the first half mile, and on reaching a T-junction turn right for Lustleigh, going right again for Cleave at the next junction. This is a high narrow road looking across and down Lustleigh valley and from it on the right the footpath starts to Lustleigh Cleave. There is parking space for several cars to tempt the energetic tourist.

Turn left into Lustleigh at the signposted junction, and drive through this scattered village with several pretty corners, one of the best being round the green by the church. Keeping the church on our left we shortly turn right at a junction for Bovey Tracey, then right again, crossing a disused railway track, finally turning left at the T-junction beyond it. This brings us to the major road, in which we turn right to rejoin our outward route at Bovey Tracey, and thence back to Newton Abbot and Torbay.

Tour two: Widecombe, Dartmeet, Buckfast Abbey

The second Dartmoor tour takes us to several celebrated villages and beauty spots, and near the end includes a visit to Buckfast Abbey. From Torquay centre and back the distance is about seventy miles. We leave from the harbour along the sea front towards Paignton and after passing Livermead House Hotel turn right for Cockington, reached in about three-quarters of a mile along a tree-lined valley. At the centre (see page 5) by the forge we turn left, passing the entrance to the church and the gardens of Cockington Court, going forward at a junction with a wider road and crossing the Ring Road into Vicarage Hill for Compton Castle. At this point we already have a distant sight of Hay Tor, Saddle Tor, and Rippon Tor.

The entrance to the splendid fortified manor-house, of which the earliest part is the restored Great Hall, is on the left and may be visited on Mondays, Wednesdays and Thursdays from April to October. The original Compton Castle was built and enlarged over several centuries by the Gilbert family and has remained in their possession, with a break in the nineteenth century, for six hundred years. The famous explorer, Sir Humphrey Gilbert, was the half-brother of Sir Walter Raleigh and his son took the name of Raleigh Gilbert. The present holder of Compton Castle is descended from these illustrious ancestors.

Continuing on the same road, go forward at all subsequent junctions, including the main Newton Abbot–Totnes road, and in about three miles descend a steep hill (1 in 5) through woods into a green valley. On the ascent go forward for Ashburton, then follow this little road to the town, crossing the bypass (A38) into it. Ashburton is a pleasant town showing many signs of its early importance as a market centre, and it has given its name to a highly-prized marble quarried locally and exported to other countries. The old houses in the main street, though of several

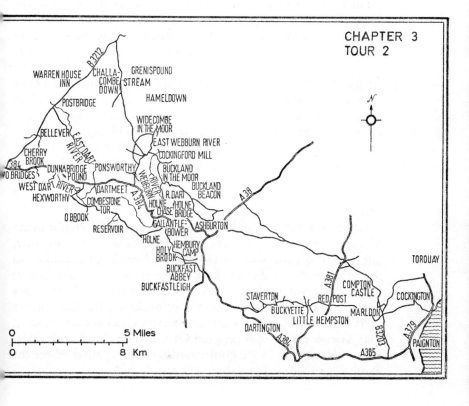

CHAPTER 3
TOUR 2

different styles, a number faced with hanging slates, are in perfect harmony. An imposing square granite conduit faces the Golden Lion inn, formerly a handsome Georgian residence.

The main street winds down to the centre, then up again, and we leave it in the dip by turning into North Street opposite the museum, noticing on our right in a few yards an intriguing house covered in hanging slates representing the four suits of playing cards. Our road runs beside the river on our left and as we leave the town we cross it for Buckland and proceed along a road lined by a wall surmounted by trees on our left and hedged on the right. As the view opens out the bare slopes of Buckland Beacon (1,281 ft) with its tor etched against the sky rise to our right.

After a lovely ride covering 3 miles, at intervals looking into Holne Chase on our left, a beech-lined road brings us into the rightly-famous Buckland in the Moor, its thatched cottages charmingly composed beside a stream cascading over rocks. Winding uphill between moss-grown walls, we drive beside the dense woods of the Georgian Buckland Court and past the church, our road high above the Webburn valley, the river here very near its confluence with the Dart. At a T-junction turn left for Widecombe down a steep hill to cross the East Webburn at Cockingford Mill, with a steeper ascent on the other side of the river to a T-junction. Here turn right for Widecombe and soon the graceful pinnacled tower of Widecombe church guides us into the village, the fame of which needs no underlining. There is a useful car park by the village green, where the village sign of course displays the grey mare carrying 'Uncle Tom Cobleigh and All'. Outside the lych gate of the interesting church is the old church house, variously used in later times as a school and almshouses.

We retrace our way for just over a mile from Widecombe in the Moor, to give it its full name, then bear right for Ponsworthy, but leave this road in about two hundred yards for a turning on the right for Postbridge and bear right once more at a subsequent fork. Now we are in the midst of moorland, the bare slopes stretching away endlessly but not colourlessly, for the brilliant gold of the dwarf gorse brightens the landscapes at most seasons. Our narrow road winds between Challacombe Down and whale-backed Hameldon as we go forward for Grimspound where the Postbridge road makes a sharp left turn.

Grimspound lies in a concentrated area of stone monuments and other remains of prehistoric inhabitation. These early settlers are known to have worked the tin mines and to have cultivated the land. It is worth parking the car by a stream three-quarters of a mile beyond the Postbridge turn to walk to Grimspound, which lies less than a quarter of a mile to the right of the road. The footpath follows the bank of the stream, no doubt the water supply for the people of this prehistoric settlement and their cattle. It consists of twenty-four hut circles, i.e. foundations of Bronze Age stone homes surrounded by a strong stone wall.

As we proceed on our way some further hut circles are visible on the left slope near another stream. Another mile and a quarter brings us to a major road, the B3212, in which we turn left for Postbridge, noticing the simple Bennett's Cross on the left shortly before we reach the Warren House inn, one of the highest inns in England, and certainly the highest on Dartmoor (1,450 ft). The original inn was built in the fourteenth century to serve the medieval tin miners in the vicinity, but the present building is little over 120 years old. It claims that its peat fire has never gone out during that time.

The road descends from here to Postbridge, in an area sometimes described as an 'oasis' near the heart of the moor, for here are fields enclosed by stone walls surmounted by beeches. Beside the road bridge over the East Dart stands the finest of the old 'clapper' bridges, believed to date from early medieval times. A quarter of a mile beyond the bridge a road leads through the forest to Bellever, where a parking space is provided near the entrance to the woods which makes an ideal picnic place, and several small surfaced roads can be explored by car or on foot before we return to the major road. This is a grand moorland road looking over the heather- and gorse-covered expanses. Half a mile after crossing the Cherry Brook the old powder mills can be seen on our right, marked by a tall chimney, and afterwards Cherry Brook Farm (now an hotel). Between this and Two Bridges, also to our right, Crockern Tor is famous as the meeting place of the Stannary court (see page 27), over which Sir Walter Raleigh presided with great efficiency and justice during his period of office.

At Two Bridges we turn left on A384 for Ashburton just short of the bridge over the West Dart. This is another splendid stretch of moorland highway looking down to the West Dart on the right. After two miles we see on the left near a group of farm buildings the circular Dunnabridge Pound, resembling the sheep pens seen in many mountain districts of Britain. A mile from the pound turn right for Hexworthy (at this point the famous beauty spot at Dartmeet is a bare half mile farther on the main road) and soon reach the bank of the West Dart, crossing it by a high-arched stone bridge.

When we reach the sign '1 in 5 hill' it is essential to engage bottom gear and continue in this gear until we have passed the Forest Inn. We shall feel the slow climb well worth while as we drive towards Holne on this high-set road and look across the beautiful Dart valley to Hameldon. We cross the pretty tumbling stream of the O Brook, which surely can claim to have the shortest name in England (though I have previously come across an I Brook to match it), then the road climbs to Combestone Tor and attains a point level with the high rocks, where there is a car park to give us leisure to enjoy a lovely bird's-eye view of Dartmeet. Thence our road is straightforward, crossing the dam of the placid Venford reservoir, fringed with larches along the shore we follow and by a small plantation of mixed conifers on the farther shore, and continuing to Holne, which is well signposted.

This important village of Holne Chase, the vast area of woodland enclosed by an elongated loop of the Dart, has an interesting church and church house, the latter now an inn and dated 1329. Charles Kingsley, the author of *Westward Ho!*, was born at the Georgian vicarage in 1819, and there is a fine memorial window to him in the church, the modern stained glass depicting in rich colours the Three Kings and the Shepherds worshipping the Christ child in the Virgin's arms, with a portrait of Kingsley above. There is a car park almost opposite the church.

We leave Holne by the road beside the Church House inn, signposted Ashburton, turning right at an ensuing т-junction, then taking a right fork (both currently unsignposted). The next junction is at a place marked on the ordnance survey map as Gallant Le Bower but, alas, there is nothing to give this evocative name point. However, for compensation there is a parking space and a sign indicating that a footpath leads from here to the ancient bridge of Holne Park. As this is a full three-quarters of a mile away, we shall probably prefer to pursue our way to Buckfast-leigh, appreciating the vista stretching ahead of us. In the National Trust property of Hembury is a prehistoric fort known as Hembury Camp, but although it abuts on the road its features are not easy to trace, except by the expert archaeologist. Beyond the camp we begin a long steep descent through woods (low gear is advisable) to cross the Holy Brook, a short distance beyond it turning left for Buckfast.

We drive under one of the old gateways into the abbey precinct, where it is well worth parking to see this great abbey, the con-ception of one man, Abbot Anscar Vonier, under whose inspira-tion the work of rebuilding the medieval Cistercian monastery was carried out by the monks within the space of twenty-five years, a truly marvellous achievement. The beautiful abbey church is an impressive Gothic building with a tall pinnacled tower, a spacious nave, and a richly decorated chancel. Recently a new chapel has been added for private prayer, an arresting modern structure of glass walls and windows with predominantly abstract designs in stained glass. Many branches of agriculture and craft industries are carried on by the monks.

We leave the abbey by a second gateway and soon join A38 in order to cross the Dart but turning off it on the other side into A384 (right). The spire of Buckfastleigh church is seen high to the right before we leave the outskirts of the village. Our road is another pleasant main one, following the bank of the Dart at first, then climbing over a hill, and we keep to it for just over two miles to a left fork signposted Staverton, which brings us in less than a mile (neglecting a turning on the left) to Staverton Bridge station. On the right is one of the oldest and finest bridges in Devon, with seven arches spanning the broad Dart. The once important mill beside it now houses a building branch of Darting-ton's activities. We do not cross the bridge but continue on our road to Staverton village and at the Sea Trout inn take the sign-posted right fork for Little Hempston, forking right again at the next junction and going over the ensuing crossroads.

We are now making for Red Post and after the first signposted fork reach a complex of junctions at the bottom of a steep hill which we need to negotiate correctly. We turn right at the first, left to cross a stream, and right on the other side to go under a railway bridge, visible ahead.   The rest of the way to Red Post is simple.   We turn right at a т-junction for Marldon and soon cross the main road at Red Post, bearing left for Marldon in about two hundred yards, and at the next crossroads go forward for Marldon and Paignton.   Thereafter we follow this road, turning left at a т-junction and going over a crossroads into Five Lanes Road, which brings us to the Ring Road, where right for Paignton and left for Torquay.

In the course of these tours we shall have seen the greater part of Dartmoor which can be covered by car, but we have not quite said farewell to the moor.   Its south-west corner is visited from Plymouth on a tour in a later chapter (see page 74).

CHAPTER FOUR

EAST OF THE EXE

THE FAME OF DEVON east of the Exe is perhaps not equal to that of other parts of the county but for all that it has a grand coastline and beautiful river valleys in addition to that of the Exe itself, to which may be added the fact that the splendid county town lies on the east bank of the river. Exeter is, of course, the obvious centre for the tours in this chapter though there are many alternatives, such as the towns along the coast, the riverside towns, and inland towns like Honiton.

Exeter must be explored in any case, from the glorious cathedral and castle ruins of its early times to the nineteenth-century public buildings and the modern rebuilding of the city centre. The cathedral is a noble essay in Beer stone, the two sturdy Norman towers admirably setting off the sumptuous west front and added porch carrying two rows of statues. Inside, the beautiful fan vaulting is notable, especially in the chancel, and the fourteenth-century choir screen is another example of fine stone carving. The soaring Bishop's Throne is a superb tribute to the art of the fifteenth-century wood carvers, while among the intriguing subjects on the misericords number 44 has a curious elephant, representing the carver's idea of an animal he had never seen. The minstrels' gallery with its row of angels playing musical instruments and the medieval clock are also fascinating to visitors.

Parts of the city walls, incorporating Roman masonry, survive, and the Norman Gate and Athelstan's Tower are all that remain of the great castle of Rougemont. The old guildhall in the High Street dates from the fourteenth century, though the added overhanging front on pillars is Elizabethan, and the decorative Mol's Coffee House in the cathedral close is another fine Elizabethan structure.

In addition to the museums and art gallery, a maritime museum is being established on the canal to exhibit old ships of international interest. The canal itself recalls the intriguing story of Countess Weir, a place known to so many motorists who drive along the Exeter bypass. In the thirteenth century Isabella de Fortibus, Countess of Devon, had the Exe blocked below Exeter to obstruct the ships of the citizens, who had unfortunately incurred her wrath. Exeter was not able to recover its prosperity as a port until the canal was constructed in the sixteenth century.

A town which does not lie on any of the routes in this chapter and deserves a visit is Crediton, a few miles to the north-west of Exeter, reached via the attractive manorial village of Newton St Cyres. Crediton was the birthplace of St Boniface, the missionary saint of the eighth century, and it was the see of a bishop until the middle of the eleventh century, and in modern times has a suffragan bishop. The beautiful red sandstone church in the Perpendicular style and its High Street of Georgian houses indicate that the town maintained its modest prosperity through the centuries.

Tour one: Hayes Barton, Lyme Regis, Ottery St Mary

The first tour, covering about eighty-five miles, follows the coast as nearly as possible as far east as Lyme Regis, just over the Dorset border. We leave Exeter by the Topsham road (A377) and there drive on to the Strand to see the lovely Dutch houses

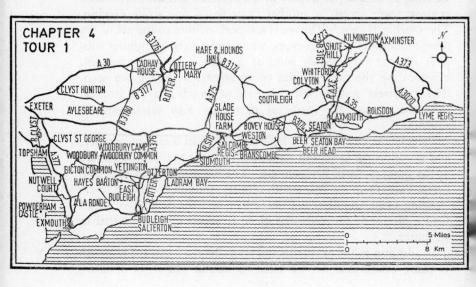

with shaped gables and the many Queen Anne and Georgian houses, including William of Orange House and Shell House, which has a pretty shell door hood. Topsham became important as a port after the obstruction of the Exe by the Countess of Devon in 1284 and it has retained its importance throughout the centuries. After returning by the lower road to the centre, we turn right on A377 towards Exmouth and soon cross the tidal river Clyst, which with the Exe forms the peninsula on which Topsham stands. Turn left by the George and Dragon hotel towards Clyst St George then bear right in a few yards for Woodbury, and shortly turn right again, on to the B3179.

At Woodbury village crossroads we turn right on the Exmouth road and continue to the main road, where we turn right for a few yards, then left for Lower Lympstone, following the estate wall of Nutwell Court and when we leave it entering Lympstone village, a rather smaller edition of neighbouring Topsham with good Georgian houses and pretty cottages. The road comes out by the estuary, where the extensive vista includes the park of Powderham Castle on the opposite shore and, to the south, Exmouth dominated by its church.

A quarter of a mile beyond the point where the road veers inland turn right, just short of a large white house, into Court-lands Lane where Exmouth is signposted. This little road brings us to the main road within a mile of Exmouth's outskirts and those who have not previously visited this popular seaside resort may wish to see it before proceeding across the main road into Summer Lane. In any case, this is a convenient point for motorists from Exmouth to join the route, turning right at the crossroads into Summer Lane. In about 150 yards, on the right, is the entrance to the unique A La Ronde, built in 1798 and modelled on an Italian villa at Ravenna. The walls are covered with shells, and seaweed and feather pictures are displayed in the gallery, which is open on weekdays from June to September and on Wednesdays in May.

The road continues to a T-junction, where we turn left for Woodbury Common, at first along a pleasant tree-lined road, then amid deeper woods, before coming out on to common land, which is, however, being changed by recent forestry. Woodbury Camp is half a mile forward from the crossroads, where a clump of pine trees at each corner together form an unmistakable landmark. As the camp, in common with all such sites selected by prehistoric man, stands at the highest point, there are immense views on all sides, and plenty of parking space to pause and enjoy them.

We return to the crossroads and turn left for East Budleigh, crossing Bicton Common to Yettington, where we turn right on the outskirts for Exmouth. The road soon crosses common land again and in three-quarters of a mile we turn left for East Budleigh but to avoid a very sharp corner we can turn left across a rough connecting track about fifty yards before reaching the signpost. The beautiful Tudor thatched farmhouse of Hayes Barton, the birthplace of Sir Walter Raleigh, lies on this minor road, and the interior is shown to visitors on weekday afternoons from June to mid-September for a small fee. It is said that the honest simplicity of the great sailor led him in later life to offer to buy back the farm at any price the then owner cared to name!

From the farm drive straight on to East Budleigh, turning left at the Sir Walter Raleigh inn, its colourful sign depicting the well-known cloak incident, to see the church, where there are wall monuments to the Raleigh family and the fine carved bench ends include one showing the Raleigh arms. From the church we return downhill between the rows of thatched cottages and beside a stream running alongside the road with bridges to the cottage gates. By the Rolle Arms we turn right and continue to Budleigh Salterton, where we follow the main road left-handed to encircle the town, gaining long views along the cliffs before we descend to the town centre.

Budleigh Salterton is as much a residential town as a holiday resort and its gracious houses, mainly Georgian, add to the tranquil atmosphere that reigns out of the holiday season. A notice on the octagonal house next to the thatched museum indicates that it was the residence of Sir John Millais, the great Victorian artist.

To resume our route, leave the main road at the war memorial at the east end of the town, driving downhill to a large car park near the shore, beyond which the river Otter reaches the sea through a narrow opening in the pebble ridge across its mouth. At the entrance to the car park turn left into Granary Lane and shortly rejoin the main road beyond the town, at the junction turning right towards East Budleigh. This road would bring us

Sheepstor church and old cross.　(Chapter 6.)

Puslinch, nr Yealmpton. (Chapter 6.)

Noss Mayo from Newton Ferrers. (Chapter 6.)

East Looe. (Chapter 6.)

to the entrance to Bicton Gardens a mile beyond East Budleigh, the beautiful Italian gardens designed by Le Nôtre, famous for the gardens of Versailles. These deserve a leisurely visit, for in addition to the gardens there is a pinetum through which a narrow-gauge railway runs and a countryside museum, all open to visitors 11 a.m. to 6 p.m. June to September and afternoons April and May.

On this occasion turn right at the first crossroads in East Budleigh along Frogmore Road, turning right again to cross the river Otter into Otterton. The old abbey mill still stands beside the river, and beyond it we look up to the blind Gothic windows at the side of the old manor-house, which incorporates part of the former monastery, and behind that rises the Norman tower of the church, the only survival of the medieval building. Otterton is another picturesque village of thatched cottages behind a stream flowing beside the main street. At the junction the turning to the right leads to Ladram Bay and we must make a detour of about a mile to see the rich red sandstone cliffs and stack rocks of the beautiful bay.

Returning to Otterton, turn right, and in a mile right again for Sidmouth. This road climbs up until it reaches the cliff top (there is a car park at the highest point) before descending the 1 in 4½ hill into Sidmouth, from which the view through the trees extends over the town up the valley of the Sid. Forward the vista is along the coast to Beer Head, where the red sandstone gives way to the chalk.

Sidmouth is a town which became fashionable in the Regency period and it is full of handsome houses dating from the early nineteenth century. It is therefore rewarding to drive through the streets of the dignified town, and to the end of the front where the Sid flows into the sea, before crossing the river for Seaton. The road continues beside a park, and we shortly turn off to the right up Salcombe Hill road, where Salcombe Regis is signposted. The hill is just as steep on this side of the Sid valley as it is on the west of Sidmouth and at the top we drive over the plateau for a short distance before forking right at the war memorial on the outskirts of Salcombe Regis to descend to the centre by the church, which looks down the steep combe towards the sea. The 'Regis' in the name dates back to Athelstan, who in the tenth century gave the manor to Exeter.

D.C.—4

At the church we turn left, and shortly right for Branscombe. This brings us to the main road in under half a mile but we soon leave it for a turning to Weston on the right by Slade House Farm, at the small village of Weston continuing to Branscombe by turning right at a т-junction. The houses of Branscombe village straggle along the sides of a deep combe which runs almost parallel with the sea before it makes a right-angled turn to Branscombe Mouth, where the stream flows through the pebble beach to the sea. The church is halfway down the valley and is believed to be on the site of a Saxon one though the earliest work existing appears to be Norman, including the massive central tower. Inside the church the three-decker pulpit, rare in the county, old box pews, and Elizabethan monuments are note-worthy. The ancient house opposite the church is the 'Living House', while a second old house, Great Seaside, a mellow farm-house near Branscombe Mouth, is in the care of the National Trust.

Retracing our way from the car park near the shore to the village, we turn right by the Mason's Arms, gay with thatched umbrellas, our road here signposted Beer and Seaton, and after climbing out of the valley take the second turning on the left, signposted Colyton. This road leads to Bovey House (now a hotel), reached along a fine avenue of mixed trees to the left of the road. The Elizabethan manor-house in grey stone with mullioned windows is entered by a round arch flanked by heraldic beasts and the adjacent farm buildings and estate cottages grouped round a sycamore-shaded green to the left complete a perfect manorial composition.

Returning to the junction, we resume our way towards Beer, famous for the pleasing cream-coloured stone quarried in the parish and seen in many south Devon buildings, of which Exeter Cathedral is the most distinguished example. As we enter the town we pass Lady Rolle's almshouses on our left and a little lower down the sixteenth-century Starre Cottage, and there are many other attractive houses along the main street, beside which a stream runs down to the sea with two quaint little conduits over it. At the foot of the street a road to the right leads to a vast cliff-top car park opposite the coastguards station, from which a track leads to Beer Head, and there are fine cliff views along the coast.

EAST OF THE EXE

We return up the main street past Starre Cottage, then turn
sharp right for Seaton, the outskirts of which are almost contiguous with those of Beer. Seaton is another favourite resort,
developed in comparatively recent times and owing a great deal
to its long front on Seaton Bay. After driving through the town
and along the front, which ends by the river Axe, continue to
the bridge and cross the wide stream, which is impeded on its
way to the sea by the pebble bar across its mouth. On the other
side we are close beside the river all the way to Axmouth, where
the road bends round into the village past the reputedly twelfth-
century Harbour inn and the church. Towards the end of the
village turn right for Stepps and later turn right for Lyme Regis
via Rousdon, left at a subsequent T-junction, and finally right on
the main road for the last mile or two into Lyme Regis.

Lyme Regis is just over the Devon border, though efforts have
been made to include it within the county and may yet succeed.
It has long been a favourite seaside resort and retains an
atmosphere reminiscent of the Georgian days when Jane Austen
stayed there and immortalized its charm in *Persuasion*. The
ancient Cobb is exactly as it was at the time of Louisa Musgrove's
dramatic fall from the steps, and the cliffs to the west just as
'romantic' even though a further landslip has occurred since Jane
Austen described them so vividly. As in her day, the undercliff
can only be explored on foot.

From Lyme take the Axminster road (A3070), turning left
on A373 after approximately three and a half miles and continuing to the town centre by the church, near which the famous
Axminster carpets were made from the mid-eighteenth century
onwards. The town took its name from a Saxon minster, long
since disappeared, and little remains of the later Newenham
Abbey by the banks of the Axe, while the imposing church has
only an arched doorway as a reminder of its Norman foundation.
We go on past the church towards Honiton for over a mile, then
turn left at a crossroads in Kilmington, passing the church, of
which only the tower remains from the original structure, and
going on for Whitford beyond the little triangular green.

This is a grand road, following the Axe valley with long views
across it, while on the right rise the lower slopes which culminate
in the Beacon on Shute Hill. At the T-junction by an attractive
cottage group in Whitford turn right, then shortly left at the Hare

and Hounds inn, for Colyton, crossing the hill between the valley of the Axe and that of the Coly. The splendid church of Colyton is evidence of the town's early importance, its central tower, crowned by a graceful octagonal top stage, a landmark for many miles. Inside, the chapel in the south aisle, enclosed by a sixteenth-century stone screen, contains monuments to the Pole family, including a fine seventeenth-century one to Sir John and Lady Elizabeth Pole with their effigies back to back under an elaborate canopy. In the north aisle the chapel, here enclosed by a Jacobean stone screen, are monuments to the Yonge family, of Great House in South Street. A fine Saxon cross discovered in this century and well restored also stands within the church. In addition to Great House, the Vicarage, and Church House, there are numerous old houses and attractive cottages to be found in the town.

We leave it by the Sidmouth and Exeter road, which starts near the market place, and continue on this road at the next junction. In less than half a mile beyond this point fork right for Southleigh along a quiet narrow lane between high banks, and keep left at the next fork. From there this little road takes us straight to Southleigh village, where we continue for Ottery St Mary up a very steep hill and over a high plateau, our road rising to over 800 ft. Various tumuli near the wayside are evidence of the prehistoric inhabitation of this downland area. Soon after going over a crossroads turn right at a major T-junction for Ottery St Mary, and after crossing the A375 at a second Hare and Hounds inn we descend a 1 in 5 hill through woods to the Otter valley and the pleasant market town.

The beautiful church of Ottery St Mary is on the Honiton road, and is unusual in having two transept towers and, inside, the lovely vaulted roofs of the nave and chancel, and the fan tracery in the north aisle are among the many interesting features. Samuel Taylor Coleridge was born in Ottery and the poet is commemorated by a plaque on the churchyard wall. There are many good Georgian houses round the church, as well as in other parts of the town, which we leave by the Exeter road past a Georgian industrial building, the old Serge Factory, a high rectangular block of the late eighteenth century.

Just over half a mile to the north of Ottery St Mary, on the Fairmile road, is the famous Elizabethan house of Cadhay, which

we must try to visit on a future occasion, though it is open only
infrequently. The mansion is built round a courtyard known as
the Court of Sovereigns, where statues of King Henry VIII and
his sovereign children, Edward, Mary, and Elizabeth, appear, one
above each entrance into the quadrangle. Cadhay is open to
visitors on Wednesday and Thursday afternoons from late July
to early September and on the Spring and Summer Bank Holidays.

After crossing the Otter river and the railway by a level
crossing, we can either bear right and thence continue to Exeter,
joining A30 for the last few miles, or take the left road for a
quieter way as far as Clyst Honiton via Aylesbeare.

Tour two: Honiton, Tiverton

The second tour, of about ninety miles, takes us to the old
market towns of Honiton and Tiverton, and to many villages
typical of east Devon. We leave Exeter by Queen Street, passing
the museum and Central railway station and following the
Crediton road (A377) left of the clock tower and right of the
Buller statue. We pass the entrance to the University as we leave
the city and continue to Cowley Bridge (about two miles from
the centre), forking right before reaching the bridge on A396 on
the Tiverton road.

The road follows the Exe to the confluence with the Culm,
then continues alongside the latter under the wooded slopes of
Stoke Woods, an attractive mixture of deciduous trees and
conifers. At Stoke Canon we enter the village by a causeway
and bridges crossing two branches of the Culm, turning right
after passing a terrace of gabled cottages on the left and the
church on the right, the latter a rebuilding but retaining its
ancient Norman font with quaint figures supporting the bowl
decorated with interlacing patterns.

Our minor road takes us through Huxham and then towards
Poltimore, but turn aside before reaching Poltimore, going
forward for Killerton at a crossroads and drive under the fine
mature trees of Danes Wood before seeing the impressive
Georgian mansion of Killerton, a mellow stone house backed by
the wooded Dolbury Hill, where there is a prehistoric earthwork
concealed among the trees. The entrance to the beautiful gardens
is beside the stables and visitors are admitted daily throughout
the year.

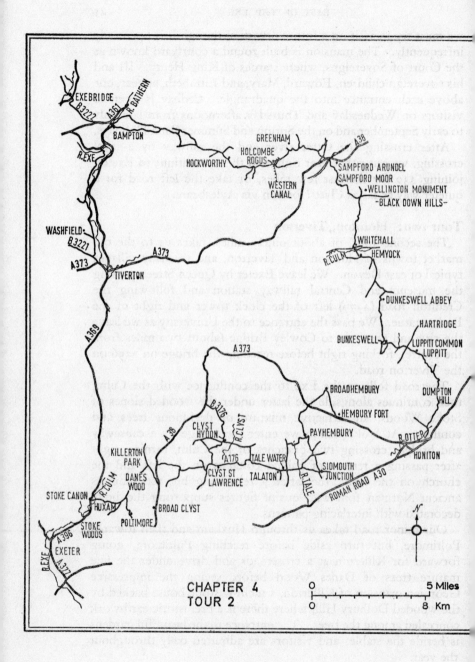

CHAPTER 4
TOUR 2

0   5 Miles

0   8 Km

A few yards beyond the gates turn right towards Broadclyst
and on reaching the main road (A38) turn sharp left towards
Taunton for three-quarters of a mile, turning right at a minor
crossroads a short distance beyond the National Trust sign marking the extensive woods to the right of the road. We now drive
through the heart of these woods and finally turn left at a junction
where Clyst St Lawrence is signposted, passing Snaffle Park,
where the woods are open to the public for riding and walking.

Shortly after the road leaves the woodland we turn right at a
T-junction, then left at a subsequent T-junction for Clyst Hydon,
now driving over a level landscape of fields broken up by mature
hedgerow timber and small orchards. Near the highest point of
the road we turn left again for Clyst Hydon, and later right into
the village past the thatched Five Bells inn and a cottage group.
The church, on the left near the bank of the Clyst at the other
end of the village, has an unusual rood turret beside the south
porch. Cross the river and after less than a mile turn right for
Talaton, continuing to the attractive village, where there are a
number of unexpectedly well preserved sculptured figures on the
church tower and turret.

In the centre of Talaton turn left where Sidmouth Junction is
signposted and after going over a crossroads and crossing the
Tale Water leave the Sidmouth Junction road for a turning on
the left signposted Payhembury and Hembury. We go forward
at a crossroads and bear left to reach Payhembury, a pleasant
village with the church in an attractive setting. The church is
entered by a wrought iron gate between tall stone pillars, and
inside the wide rood screen, richly embellished, is worth seeing.

With the church on our right we continue through the village
and shortly turn right for Broadhembury, thereafter following
the signposts to the latter, crossing the main road by the park of
The Grange, an Elizabethan mansion with Georgian additions
which can be seen from the road.

Broadhembury is outstanding even among the renowned
villages of Devon. Thatched and washed cottages line the main
street, fanning out as they build up to form a spacious centre in
front of the church and the Tudor Drewe Arms beside the church
gate. Bear left by the church, noting the tower stair turret capped
by a spirelet, then after half encircling it turn right into a lesser
road, following this to the main road. Here we turn left, in a few

yards passing below the mighty Hembury Fort on a promontory nearly 900 ft above sea-level, a prehistoric camp a quarter of a mile long with three ramparts divided by ditches.

From Hembury we descend into Honiton, crossing the modern bypass by a fly-over. Now that the bypass has relieved the pressure of traffic in the town it is possible to see the mile-long High Street of Honiton (on the line of a Roman road) by driving along it. The best plan is to turn right on the Exeter road and drive as far as the almshouses of St Margaret's Hospital, a medieval leper hospital which was later refounded for old people, and then return from there through the whole length of the town, noting its homogeneous appearance due to the mid-eighteenth-century rebuilding after the town was virtually destroyed by fire. It became an important coaching stage and there are many handsome inns, past and present, recalling this era. Notice particularly the Manor House near the centre and Marwood House at the far end. Honiton is still famous for lace and pottery, and both are to be found in the High Street, the pottery announcing that visitors are welcome.

We continue on A30 beyond the end of the town for only a few yards, then turn left for Luppitt and Dunkeswell, recrossing the bypass and soon the river Otter, here flowing amid a beautiful landscape rising to Dumpdon Hill, another eminence crowned by a large prehistoric fort planted with trees. Take the next turning on the right for Luppitt, a narrow road running below Dumpdon Hill and then the long Hartridge. The village of Luppitt straggles up a very steep hill, with the church on the left. It is possible to park beyond it and walk back to see the interior of the cruciform church, particularly the rare oak 'cradle' roof (two mighty beams crossing at the centre and waggon-roofs over the nave, chancel and transepts). Two Norman survivals are the carved pillar piscina and the font, which shows pagan warriors attacking the head of (possibly) a Christian saint.

At the top of the hill beyond the church fork left, after the highest point of the road (833 ft) crossing Luppitt Common on the way to Dunkeswell. Soon after going over a crossroads the road plunges steeply through park land into a deep combe, crossing a stream which widens into an ornamental lake on the right, and climbs up equally steeply to high-set Dunkeswell, first going down into another combe before the final climb to the village. There bear right and after passing the church turn right for Dunkeswell Abbey along a ridge road overlooking a wooded countryside. A fragment of the old abbey survives near the nineteenth-century church, the spire of which appears above the treetops as we proceed towards Hemyock. At a T-junction we turn left, thence following the signposts to Hemyock. There we turn right by the church on the Tiverton road, noting some fragments of masonry on the left which mark the site of the ancient castle, and in half a mile turn right for Whitehall, then after a level-crossing turn left, then right.

Now we keep right to skirt an outlier of the imminent Blackdown Hills, coming close to the spur which is surmounted by the Wellington monument. The road goes over woodland and common as it crosses the shoulder and from the highest point there is a magnificent view over the fertile Vale of Taunton Deane. At a wide crossroads we turn sharp left into the minor road for Sampford Moor, descending through woods. At the bottom of the steep hill we turn left and continue through Sampford Moor on the Wellington road, then turning left for Sampford Arundel. Here we bear right by the church and left under a railway bridge at the end of the village, crossing the main road (A38) and at once turning left opposite the Beam Bridge hotel. In a quarter of a mile we go forward over a crossroads for Greenham, and at the next crossroads turn left for Holcombe Rogus, which is from this point reliably signposted. We drive through the village on the Hockworthy road, which brings us to the splendid Tudor Holcombe Court and adjacent church. We can get a good view of the house and dovecote through the gates, and can see the monuments to the Bluett family, who held Holcombe for about four hundred years, in the church, but to see the house it is necessary to make an appointment.

We continue to the hillside village of Hockworthy and uphill beyond it, then forward at the next crossroads for Bampton, which is from now on well signposted. The countryside between here and the Batherm valley is high downland, divided into extensive fields and with few trees, before we descend to river level and cross the Batherm into Bampton, an ancient market town with a medieval church, but otherwise showing few signs of its antiquity.

At this point an interesting detour can be made by leaving the town on B3222 for Exebridge, little more than two miles distant, to visit a trout hatchery. The hatchery is situated along a narrow turning to the right on the other side of the bridge. On weekdays during normal working hours visitors are shown the fish in their various stages of growth, from the smallest fry to mature specimens ready to be supplied for the restocking of rivers.

From the centre of Bampton recross the Batherm and follow its course on A396 to cross the river in a mile just above its confluence with the Exe. We cross the Exe in turn in a quarter of a mile by a small modern bridge, reached by an unsignposted narrow road on the left. This is the beginning of a minor road which follows the course of the river all the way to Tiverton on the opposite bank from that taken by the main road. It climbs up very steeply and is narrow at times, but it goes through beautiful woodlands and gives wonderful views across the river in the valley below.

At the first signposted junction we turn left towards Cove but do not cross the river to Cove when we come to the bridge by a thatched cottage. The right turn for Washfield is a very sharp one, however, so we may find it easier to turn by crossing the bridge and then recrossing it. From now on we keep as close to the river as possible without crossing it and for most of the way we are above and very near its course. As we approach Tiverton we join first the B3221, then enter on the main road (A373), continuing to the town centre.

Tiverton is an important town at the junction of the Exe and Lowman and is full of interesting old buildings, of which the noble church is the most impressive. The south porch and the Greenway chapel are lavishly decorated with rich carving, and the graceful red sandstone tower rises to 90 ft. John Greenway, a rich medieval merchant, also founded almshouses in the town, the sixteenth-century chapel of which survives. The ruins of the castle lie beyond the church, and the famous Blundell's School is on the eastern outskirts. From Tiverton we return to Exeter on A396.

Tour three: Exe and Culm valleys

The next tour is a shorter one of about sixty miles, exploring the country of the Exe and Culm valleys. We leave Exeter by the same route as for the previous tour and continue on A377 to Cowley bridge (about two miles from the centre), a quarter of a

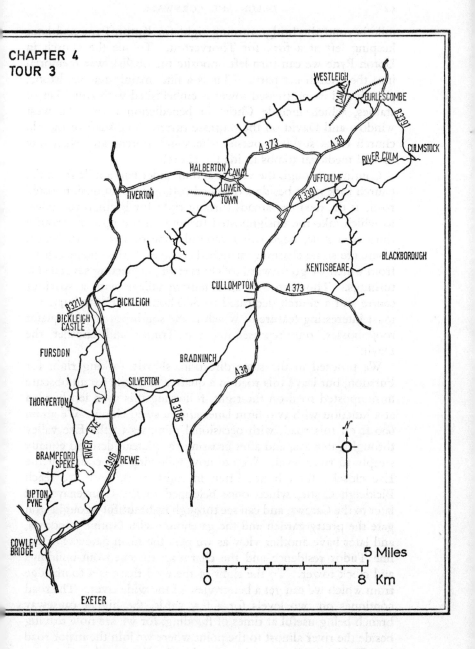

WESTLEIGH

CANAL

BURLESCOMBE

B3391

CULMSTOCK

A 373

A 38

RIVER CULM

HALBERTON   CANAL

UFFCULME

TIVERTON   LOWER TOWN

B 3391

BLACKBOROUGH

KENTISBEARE

CULLOMPTON   A 373

B3214

BICKLEIGH

BICKLEIGH CASTLE

FURSDON

BRADNINCH   A38

SILVERTON

THORVERTON   B 3185

RIVER EXE

BRAMPFORD SPEKE   A 396   REWE

UPTON PYNE

N

COWLEY BRIDGE

0   5 Miles

0   8 Km

EXETER

mile beyond the bridge turning right for Upton Pyne and later keeping left at a fork for Thorverton. To see the church in Upton Pyne we can turn left opposite the obelisk war memorial into the church car park. This is a fine, mainly red sandstone, church and its buttressed tower is embellished with a number of statues, which include Christ in benediction above the west window and David on the staircase turret. The shaft of the old church cross survives outside the south porch, and there are several medieval tombs inside the church.

Continue through the village and in under half a mile from the church fork right beside a thatched cottage into an unsignposted road, at the next crossroads turning right for Brampford Speke, to which take the unsignposted turning on the right in about a third of a mile, negotiating carefully one or two sharp bends. There are some charming thatched cottages in the village centre, from which we go forward to Thorverton, neglecting several side turnings. Thorverton is an extensive village with a spacious centre and a church dedicated to St Thomas of Canterbury, the most interesting feature of which is the south porch with quaint roof bosses, one representing the Trinity and another the Devil.

We proceed in the same direction, shortly forking right for Fursdon, but leave this road in a quarter of a mile for an obscure unsignposted road on the right, following this road left-handed at a junction with two farm lanes after a steep climb. We attain 600 ft on this road, with occasional glimpses to the Exe valley through gateways, and after crossing the plateau descend equally steeply to river level. We are now following the course of the Exe closely, though not often in sight of it, until we reach Bickleigh Castle, which once belonged to the Courtenays and later to the Carews, and can see through its beautiful wrought iron gate the pretty garden and the gatehouse with Gothic windows, and later have another view as we pass the main gateway of the fine Tudor residence and the charming thatched out-buildings and clock tower. To the right of the road there is a footbridge from which we can get a better view of the wide river. The road continues on two levels for a few yards, the higher causeway branch being useful at times of flooding, for we are now driving beside the river almost to the point where we join the major road into Bickleigh village, at last crossing the Exe into it.

Bickleigh is a lovely village of thatched cottages beside the Exe, here spanned by a fine old bridge, and is beloved of fishermen and holiday-makers alike. The Church of St Mary is of the Decorated Gothic period and has a number of interesting monuments to the Carew family. Take the steep hill to the left of the church, continuing for over two miles to a staggered crossroads, there going forward. At the next T-junction we turn left, descending to cross a stream, then go forward at a crossroads at the top of the hill for Halberton (from this point Tiverton is only two miles to the left).

As we drop down into Halberton the view extends forward towards the Brendon Hills of Somerset, and in the valley we turn left on the Tiverton road and cross a disused railway. We turn right at the T-junction in the Lower Town of Halberton, and right again by a stone wall along 'Church Path' to see the handsome Church of St Andrew. This is another red sandstone structure in the Decorated style but with Perpendicular windows and other interior features, in particular the beautiful rood screen and pulpit of similar date, both richly carved.

We resume our road through Halberton and turn right on A373 at the T-junction, leaving the main road after a quarter of a mile by a sharp left unsignposted turning and shortly crossing a canal. In another mile we turn right at a T-junction and follow this road for three and a half miles to Westleigh, passing through a series of hamlets on our way, and as we approach Westleigh blue lias quarries are a dominating theme. This quarry village lies mainly off the road and we go straight on and take the first right turning beyond the village, recrossing the canal and after going over the railway soon arrive at Burlescombe. Here we shall find another fine medieval church with its original rood screen, and the nave and aisles have waggon roofs with carved angels on the rafters.

Go on past the church and in just over half a mile come to A38, in which we turn left but soon leave it for B3391 on the right, where Culmstock is signposted. This road takes us directly to Culmstock, a high level road which looks across on the left to Blackdown Common, and in the pleasant riverside town we cross the Culm and go forward to Uffculme. At Uffculme we recross the river into the centre by the church, which has an exceptionally fine rood screen stretching across the whole width of the nave and aisles. The major road turns left at the church, and we turn left again near the end of the village by a Gothic-style chapel and once more cross the Culm as we continue in as straight a course as possible southward to Kentisbeare.

We arrive at Kentisbeare by the church, which has a west tower and stair turret decorated with red and grey chequerwork. The Old Priest's House, dated 1300, can be seen in daylight hours at any time of the year by application to the occupant. From the church continue uphill and take the right fork (the left branch indicates Blackborough) and thence follow the signposts to Cullompton.

Situated at a commanding position on the Culm and the main Bristol–Exeter road, Cullompton shows many signs of its importance as a market and industrial town, with its fine houses in the main street and majestic church just off it. Notice in particular the Manor House hotel and its beautiful double shell door hood. The church has a rich tower of the 'Somerset' type, and inside beautiful carving on the timber roof and on the rood screen, both coloured and gilded, while there is magnificent fan tracery in the south aisle.

We continue along the main street with the church on our left and near the end fork right for Bradninch beside the Cullompton hotel. The road climbs up to Bradninch, an ancient borough on a spur above the Culm, and we drive along its wide tree-lined main street lined with pleasant houses which were once mostly thatched. The tall-towered church has one of the more elaborate rood screens, with lavish carving and fan vaulting.

At the bottom of the High Street go forward for Silverton and at a crossroads turn right where Silverton is again signposted, continuing to a major road T-junction where once more turn right. After that turn away from Silverton, taking a lesser road to the left for Thorverton and going forward until at a crossroads we turn left for Exeter and in a mile reach the main road near Rewe, and so follow the Culm back along the valley road to its junction with the Exe.

NORTH DEVON

NORTH DEVON may lack the soft climate of the south but it has compensations in its superb coastal scenery. Ilfracombe is perhaps not quite to North Devon what Torquay is to South Devon but it is strategically placed and from its central position commands the coast as far as the Somerset and Cornish borders from the tourist's point of view, while exploration of the hinterland is just as convenient. Add to this fact the grand cliff walks adjoining the town and the ample accommodation of all kinds, and it becomes easy to understand why Ilfracombe has become such a popular resort. The medieval church is a fine one, and though there are few old buildings in the town, the old manor-house at Chambercombe can be seen by visitors daily from Easter to mid-October.

The following tours are routed from Ilfracombe, but they are just as conveniently followed from other centres, such as Barnstaple and Bideford, or the many smaller resorts on the routes.

Tour one: Taw and Torridge valleys

The first tour is a long one covering almost 130 miles from Ilfracombe (just over 100 from Barnstaple) exploring the Taw and Torridge valleys and the many small towns and picturesque villages on and near their banks. The tour could, of course, be divided by following each river as a separate tour and returning to base by the direct road.

We leave Ilfracombe by the Barnstaple road (B3230), which leaves the Lynton road at a fork and takes us directly to Barnstaple via Bittadon, Milltown, and Muddiford, following closely the Bradiford river through its wooded valley. If we have not previously seen Barnstaple we must spare time to look at its historic buildings, in particular Queen Anne's colonnaded Walk with a charming statue of Queen Anne, the Penrose Almshouses, also with a colonnade, the classical guildhall, the nearby Butchers'

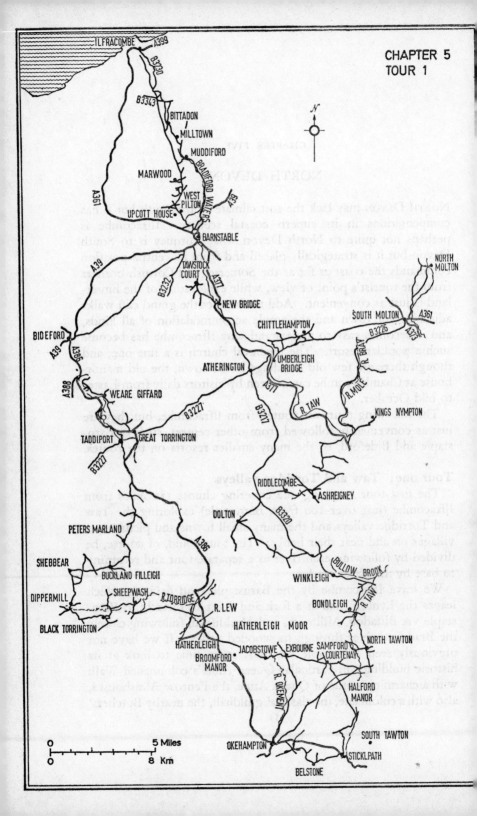

CHAPTER 5
TOUR 1

Malpas Ferry, nr Truro. (Chapter 7.)

Polperro. (Chapter 6.)

Truro Cathedral. (Chapter 7.)

St Mawes Castle. (Chapter 7.)

Row, and the parish church. Only the mound of the castle remains, now covered in trees. Pilton must also be visited for its fine houses, its historic school, pleasant almshouses, and its impressive church with notable monuments of the Chichester family. However, Barnstaple and its environs are so interesting that they deserve a much longer visit than can be made during a day's tour, so it would be preferable to defer our sightseeing for a future occasion.

We cross the ancient Taw bridge of sixteen arches out of Barnstaple then turn sharp left for Tawstock on the other side of the railway, guided towards our destination by a prospect tower, and are soon within the wooded park of Tawstock Court. After driving under an estate arch and passing a gated drive, follow a high wall round to the left to go through a gateway leading to the church and house, passing on our way the sixteenth-century gatehouse, all that remains of the Tudor mansion. The church of St Peter is well worth a visit for the magnificent monuments of the Bourchier and Wrey families, which were united by marriage. The recumbent effigies of William Bourchier, the third Earl of Bath, and his wife are especially resplendent in their elaborate setting, and the simple standing figure in white marble of the fifth Earl's wife has an appealing charm. The house, which was rebuilt in Georgian times, is less satisfying for it followed the then popular style, with exaggerated battlements and 'Gothic' windows.

On returning to the gateway, which appears to be guarded by stone dogs on its pillars, drive straight down into the village and turn left for Newbridge, where we join the main road for little over two miles, with the Taw to our left, before forking right for Atherington. Here again is a fine church, with a tall slender tower and stair turret rising above it, and inside an exquisitely carved rood screen and medieval armoured effigies, as well as a Tudor knight with his two wives and twelve children. With the church on our left we follow the road to Umberleigh Bridge, taking the right fork steeply down to cross the main road by the Rising Sun, and this time cross the wide Taw and turn left on the other side for Chittlehampton. The signposts guide us in two miles to the spacious centre of this delightful village, with its pump and pretty thatched cottages overlooked by the glorious 'Somerset' tower of the church, showing the typical rich carving on the belfry windows and elaborate pinnacles. Beyond the village bear right at the first fork for South Molton, thereafter following the signposts into the town, the church tower acting as a beacon.

South Molton, high above the river Mole, shows every sign of its importance as an ancient market town, the focal point of many roads from every direction. Its long High Street is flanked by fine houses of various periods and where it becomes the wide market place we find the classical guildhall of 1743, on the front of which is a bust of Hugh Squier 'Our Great Benefactor, 1625–1710', founder of the town school. Next to the guildhall is the mid-Victorian market house and assembly room in a similar classical style, while the Medical Hall on the island site also has a classical flavour with its Ionic columns.

North Molton, reached along a grand wooded valley, also stands high above the river a few miles to the north, and retains its old court house beside the church. It has won fame for its breed of North Devon beef cattle, the 'Red Rubies', named for their unmistakable glowing red-brown colour. We shall frequently see them grazing in the pasture fields during our travels in North Devon. Our route continues from South Molton, however, so this is a detour to be included if time allows.

From South Molton's centre take South Street and turn right outside the town on B3226, signposted Exeter, and follow this lovely wooded road above the Mole valley to King's Nympton, later signposted, after two miles crossing the river, and at King's Nympton going on for the railway station. On reaching the main road, A377, at the Fortescue Arms, we rejoin the Taw valley and turn right to cross the river. Almost immediately leave the main road for a turning on the left signposted Burrington, a single-track lane through woods which keeps close to the winding Taw. At the next T-junction turn left towards Chulmleigh, then shortly right for Ashreigney on a straight road that turns away from the river valley and climbs over the plateau. In two miles we arrive at a complex junction, where we bear right then forward for Riddle-combe, going on for the latter steeply down hill (low gear is necessary), crossing two brooks, then ascending to the hilltop village past its pseudo-Gothic church. At the top of the village turn right, and in a few yards left, for Dolton, and in just over a mile left again at a T-junction, shortly turning right opposite a garage for the final mile into Dolton.

Dolton is another village of lovely cottages, where we take the left fork at the war memorial to see the church and the unique font composed of two sections of a Saxon Cross, one placed upside down on the other, with beautiful interlacing patterns and animals in the characteristic Celtic style. We return from the church past the Union hotel and turn right, right again at a crossroads, and left at a subsequent crossroads for Winkleigh. Next, go forward at a crossroads, left at a fork, and over a runway of a disused aerodrome, at its end turning right on B3220, and right again into the high-set village dominated by its tall church tower. We keep the church on our left as we half encircle the village to rejoin B3220 and turn right towards Crediton. Now we are following the valley of the tributary Bullow brook to its junction with the Taw valley, turning right for Bondleigh short of the river crossing. Very soon we turn left along a narrow road which runs parallel to the Taw and brings us to Bondleigh at a T-junction, where we turn left to cross the Taw by an old bridge. Bondleigh church is a quarter of a mile to the right from the T-junction, and has a number of Norman features, including the south doorway with a typical lamb and birds tympanum, the font, and two richly ornamented capitals.

After crossing the Taw turn right immediately for North Tawton, climbing through woodland and over high ground to the village, placed well above the river level. It is an interesting old market town and in the centre, apart from the church, has one link with its medieval past, the fifteenth-century doorway and bay window with carved stone mullions of a house opposite the Victorian town hall. Turn right at the clock tower and beyond the village cross the Taw for the last time on the outward journey on our way to Sampford Courtenay, which we reach via B3216 in under a mile and a half. At the sixteenth-century 'New' inn we turn right to see the exceptionally lovely cottages along the road to the church.

We must return to the main road and there retrace our route for only a quarter of a mile before turning right for South Tawton. On our way we cross a major road and see an out-standing thatched farmhouse on our right and Halford Manor on our left, dated 1615 over the porch. Just over half a mile farther turn right for Sticklepath, keeping to the west bank of the Taw (South Tawton is on the east bank and is visited on another tour —see page 28). On reaching A30 turn right at the Taw River inn, then left for Belstone, driving between bracken-covered slopes and the Taw river deep in a wooded glen to the left, then beneath the steep escarpment of Belstone Cleave rising towards Cosdon's summit.

At Belstone's village green, marked by a monolith and stocks, we keep the church on our left and pass the 'Telegraph Office', bearing right at an unsignposted fork, thereafter following the signposts to Okehampton, turning left on A30 to enter the town. Okehampton is a large market town with a fine castle just outside the town near the banks of the wooded Okement river below the Tavistock road (A30). There is a car park near the market house reached by a turning from Fore Street opposite the imposing White Hart inn and beside the seventeenth-century town hall, a handsome classical building with an oriel window. The chapel of St James is also in Fore Street, but only its tower is medieval.

We have already passed our turning on the way into the town, so we must return over the river to this point, signposted B3217 Exbourne, taking care to turn sharp left into Northfield Road, at the end of which we turn right, driving beside the Okement along the well-timbered valley. Where the fields are ploughed the dark red soil characteristic of this area is revealed. In the village we pass the attractive Red Lion inn and the granite church, then turn right by the village hall, and right again at Town End, finally right once more on reaching the major road to Jacobstowe and Hatherleigh.

Jacobstowe, a mile distant, is a village of pretty cottages grouped near its mellow church, which we pass on the Hatherleigh road and drive beside the park of nearby Broomford Manor, where many graceful exotics are set off by the oaks and other native trees. This tree-lined road joins the main road into Hatherleigh in just over two miles, but we need not take this, for there is a minor road on the right over Hatherleigh Moor which is a more interesting approach to the town. We turn into this without touching the main road and drive over the moor, where there is a monument to a local hero of Balaclava. A tradition survives that the moor belongs to the poor of the parish. Baring-Gould quotes an old rhyme:

I, John of Gaunt,
  Do give and do grant
  Hatherleigh Moor
  To Hatherleigh poor,
    For evermore.

The town itself is no less ancient, and evidence of its antiquity is
on every side. Our road enters Higher Street, so that we are able
to drive down the length of the exceptionally pleasing main
street, crossing into High Street as we approach the centre and
finally into Market Street, where on the corner is the thatched
George inn, dated 1450, with a graceful balcony above the
entrance. The church near the market place has a five-stage
tower crowned by a spire. We turn uphill with the church on
our left, bearing left at the top of the street for Great Torrington,
but soon leave this road for a left turning to Sheepwash. The
road dips to cross the railway and the river Lew just above its
confluence with the Torridge and ascends above the Torridge
valley, never far from the course of the winding river. When we
reach river level we cross it by Sheepwash bridge and drive up to
the village, a harmonious composition of cottages of similar
design round a central square. Beyond the church turn left for
Black Torrington, left again at a T-junction to recross the
Torridge and in the village bear right to the church, well worth
seeing for its fine carved waggon roof and bench ends, monolithic
granite pillars with carved capitals and bases, and pink-washed
walls. Its most unusual feature is the floor of encaustic tiles,
wonderfully preserved since medieval times.

From the church entrance we courageously go forward in the
road marked 'Steep hill 1 in 5' which, however, holds no terrors
if we use a low gear. Go forward for Shebbear at the first
signposted junction and turn right for Dippermill at the second,
where we cross a pretty reach of the Torridge. Thereafter we
proceed to Shebbear amid pastoral landscapes, there pausing at
the church to look at the Norman south doorway with its beak-
heads, human and animal heads. We leave the spacious centre by
the Bideford road, passing the Devil's Stone inn, its name derived
from a rock in the village believed to have had a supernatural
origin.

Buckland Filleigh is signposted forward at the next two crossroads and we drive through an extensive wooded estate and bear

left after crossing a stream. At the next T-junction turn left for
Peters Marland, but at a chapel turn right for Torrington, joining
a major road in about a mile and a half, there turning left, and,
shortly after going over a level-crossing, join the main Torrington
road (A386). We turn off this road before reaching the town,
however, to drive through Taddiport, the compact little village
on the south bank facing Torrington, where there is a fine view
across the Torridge to Castle Hill. Near the river stands the tiny
chapel of a leper hospital which has long since vanished, and after
noting this we cross the beautiful three-arched bridge and climb
the hill into Torrington.

Torrington is wonderfully situated at the top of a cliff rising
straight from the Torridge, with a superb view from Castle Hill.
Exploring the town is made easy by the refreshingly intelligent
signposting and we shall find the charming Pannier Market in the
classical style, with Ionic columns, pediment and cupola, the
rebuilt Georgian town hall retaining the classical style, the
gabled Black Horse inn, dated 1681, and Palmer House, built in
1752, which had the distinction of being visited by Dr Johnson
and Sir Joshua Reynolds in its heyday.

To continue on our way; from the Castle Hill car park drive
along a gracious Georgian street then turn right for Bideford,
right again at a T-junction, and opposite the spired parish church
turn left for Weare Giffard and Bideford. The road passes the
entrance to Dartington glassworks, where visitors are invited to
see the whole process, from glass-blowing to the finished article.
Parties are taken round on most days at twelve noon and one
o'clock. We soon fork left and drive up a lime avenue, reaching
the riverside village of Weare Giffard in about a mile and a half.
Weare Giffard Hall and church lie to the right at the far end of the
straggling village and we can get a glimpse of the beautiful old
mansion, its later additions blending harmoniously with the
fifteenth-century gatehouse. The church just beyond the Hall
has good wood carving and some interesting monuments of the
Fortescue and Giffard families, one with special appeal being of
two seventeenth-century kneeling couples with numerous children
in separate little groups all round them, the whole representing
several generations of Fortescues.

It is time now to make for Bideford and we continue to the next
river crossing and turn right on reaching the main Bideford road

on the other side for the last two miles into this historic town beside the ancient and lovely bridge of twenty-four arches spanning the broad Torridge. The many handsome houses in the town bear witness to its prosperity through the ages, though the parish church was rebuilt in the nineteenth century. Cross the bridge to the delightfully named East-the-Water, turn left on A39 briefly, and leave it after a quarter of a mile by turning right into Old Barnstaple Road. This is a very pleasant and quiet direct road to Barnstaple, passing through one or two hamlets and giving splendid views ahead to the Taw estuary at two high crossroads. At a T-junction on the outskirts we turn left and at the main road (A39) right into Barnstaple, and thence back to Ilfracombe.

A pleasant and direct alternative to the major road is to take the Lynton road at the clock tower, then turn left for Pilton, there bearing left past a group of almshouses, and continue on this road. After the entrance to Upcott House on the left fork right for Marwood and soon after driving through the hamlet of Prixford cross a stream in the village of Marwood, where it is worth a short detour on the left to the church down a delightful lane lined with hydrangeas and roses. We return from the church as far as the nearby Georgian house and resume our road by either lane, turning left for Ilfracombe.

Tour two: Lynton, Lynmouth

Our second tour is a shorter one, covering approximately seventy miles, along the coast to Lynton and Lynmouth and across Exmoor, visiting Arlington Court, the historic home of the Chichesters, on the way back.

Leave Ilfracombe by the Lynton road, A399, which soon rises high above the town to give some of the finest views over it to the surrounding cliffs and rocks. We dip down again to go through Chambercombe and Hele and pass the rock-girt cove of Hele Bay. When we are level with the coastguards station we again have typical North Devon coast views in each direction. After driving through a sycamore avenue beside Watermouth Cove, with Watermouth Castle, a pretentious Georgian Gothic structure, above us on our right, we turn right at the Castle Mill for Berrynarbor. This little road follows the course of the stream which flows down the pretty wooded Sterridge valley, at one point widening into a lake. The valley can be followed all the way, but on this occasion continue into Berrynarbor, marked by the tall church tower which we see on the hill ahead.

Drive through the village streets lined by many attractive houses and cottages and turn left for Combe Martin after passing the church. Rejoin the coast road at Sandy Bay and continue on it to Combe Martin, rounding its cove (where there is a car park) and driving through the long village which straggles up the valley of the river Umber. Combe Martin became important when silver mines were worked in the district from the fourteenth to the sixteenth centuries. We follow the course of the Umber beyond the village, continuing on the main road until we reach a turning on the left signposted Trentishoe. Thereafter follow the signposts to Hunter's Inn, entering the Exmoor National Park marked by the sign bearing a stag's head at Stony Corner. The road climbs a saddle between Holdstone Down and Trentishoe Down, both over a thousand feet, and as we descend we have a superb view of the coast forward and to our left across the Bristol Channel to South Wales. Keep right where a rough road leads forward to Trentishoe church and descend a steep winding road into a densely wooded valley, following a river which joins the Heddon at Hunter's Inn.

We turn left at the inn for Martinhoe, but if we have not

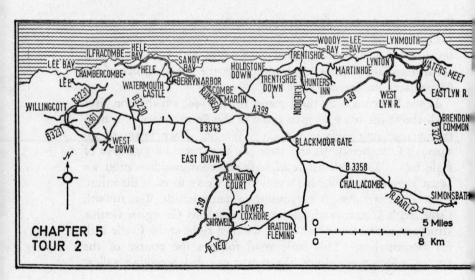

CHAPTER 5
TOUR 2

previously driven up the beautiful Heddon valley it is worth making a detour as far as the point where the road turns away from the river near the end of the woods before we continue on the route from Hunter's Inn to Martinhoe. We are climbing steeply out of the valley on this minor road, negotiating a steep hairpin bend on the way up, and at the top arrive at Martinhoe. There keep the simple village church and church house on our left and from our high open road look down on Woody Bay and along the coast. Go forward for Woody Bay and Valley of the Rocks, and at the next signpost turn left for Woody Bay and Toll Road, rounding a hairpin bend and descending through oak woods, crossing a cascading stream among ferns. (If not using toll road we keep straight on and reach Lynton by the alternative road.)

It is necessary to stress that this toll road is a narrow road on a cliff ledge with few passing places, so that it is important to drive with caution. But it is a beautiful drive through the trees which are the glory of Woody Bay and worth attempting, preferably not in the busiest part of the summer season. The toll road ends at Lee Bay after another sharp hairpin bend. Here there is a car park beside the beach. The extensive buildings of Lee Abbey stretch across the hillside above the bay and we drive past the west end by the gatehouse. The tower on the cliff above the bay was built at the same time as the Abbey, a nineteenth-century one.

In a short distance we enter the Valley of the Rocks, a unique landscape of tors and tumbled boulders with the valley running between bracken-covered slopes. A big car park and refreshments are available for those who wish to spend an hour or so in these rugged surroundings and take the remarkable cliff walk through the rocks on the sea side. We continue into Lynton, a popular resort since Victorian times with a number of hotels, passing the Tudor-style town hall (late Victorian), and leaving by the Lynmouth road, a precipitous descent with three escape roads!

We reach the harbour of this famous holiday village, ideally placed at the foot of the beautiful wooded gorge of the East and West Lyn rivers, its cottages climbing up the hillside in a most pleasing composition, and there take A39 up the valley where Blackmoor Gate is signposted, riding above the East Lyn, which runs deep in its woodland setting. After a mile and a half we come to a car park for Watersmeet (not the meeting of the East and West Lyn but the East Lyn and a tributary), which is reached by a footpath, and half a mile farther, beyond a parking space beside the river, we cross the tributary river by a new bridge, in sight of the picturesque old one with the river rushing over rocks underneath, our way signposted Simonsbath (B3223).

There is now a striking transition from the wooded valley scenery to the bare heather-clad moors of Brendon Common and Exmoor. Near the highest point of our road (1,437 ft) we cross the Exe within one mile of its source and descend gradually for about a mile and a half to Simonsbath, there turning right for Challacombe on B3358. This road runs above the Barle valley after keeping close to the river for the first half mile and after five miles over typical Exmoor landscapes we reach Challacombe, going forward at the pretty colour-washed Black Venus inn for Blackmoor Gate, but instead of turning towards Blackmoor Gate at the next T-junction (about two miles from Challacombe) turn left for Brayford, turning right after another two miles for Bratton Fleming at a crossroads. We bear right when we reach the village outskirts and drive through the long descending main street, which commands fine views.

Continue downhill on the Barnstaple road, with a deep valley on our right leading to the Yeo valley, and when we reach the latter we turn right for Loxhore, crossing the tributary stream into the woods along the course of the Yeo, which is soon visible on our left. Neglecting a turning to Lower Loxhore on our right and a left one to Shirwell, we go forward on the Parracombe road for half a mile to Loxhore, where we leave the river and climb up to the plateau, passing the church turn on our left.

At the summit fork left for Arlington, descending a rhododendron-lined road which brings us in a mile to the village, where we turn right for Arlington Court, the lovely Regency house of the Chichester family, which in addition to the period furniture and various interesting collections, retains the splendid model ships bequeathed by Miss Rosalie Chichester. The house, now in the care of the National Trust, is open to visitors daily (except Saturdays) from April to mid-October, and there is a large car park opposite the entrance.

Continue on the same road downhill, turning left on reaching the main road, the A39, then right over the Yeo for East Down in less than half a mile, and right again over a tributary stream to reach the village. We pass the church and manor-house on our left and turn left just beyond it, right at the next junction, left in about two hundred yards, then the way is straightforward for a mile and a half. This brings us to another T-junction, where we turn right, then left in a quarter of a mile for West Down. Thence we have another straightforward three-mile stretch, crossing two roads, at the end of which we turn left for a straight mile and a quarter to West Down. Here the Church of St Calixtus is interesting for its coloured timber effigy of Sir John Stowford, who was born in 1290, and is wearing his robes as sergeant-at-law. Another striking monument is the seventeenth-century upright one with half-length figures of Francis Isaac and his wife.

We return from the church to the road for Mortehoe and continue on this as far as Willingcott, crossing the main road (A361) after half a mile, and turn right at a railway arch on to a wider road. Turn right again in less than half a mile, where Ilfracombe is signposted, then shortly left for Lee. This is a pretty village on Lee Bay, a favourite beach for Ilfracombe visitors, with a pleasant garden beside the stream and a car park near the bridge. We return from there to the junction past the delightful thatched 'Old Maids Cottage' for the return to Ilfracombe.

Tour three: Hartland Point, Quay

The last tour of the chapter visits one of Devon's highlights in majestic coastal scenery, Hartland Point and Quay. It covers almost 125 miles but is well worth the effort, and here again the tour can be shortened if necessary.

Leave Ilfracombe by A361 for Barnstaple, turning right on B3343 for Mortehoe at the roundabout two miles from the centre. From that point we have only to follow the signposts to Mortehoe, driving over a plateau then dropping down through the old village to the newer resort of Woolacombe with its wonderful sweep of golden sands protected by Morte Point to the north and Baggy Point to the south and looking across to Lundy Island. The promontory ending at Morte Point is now in the care of the National Trust, and it is interesting to note that 150 acres of this land were given as a memorial to her parents by Miss Rosalie Chichester, the last owner of Arlington Court, visited on the previous tour.

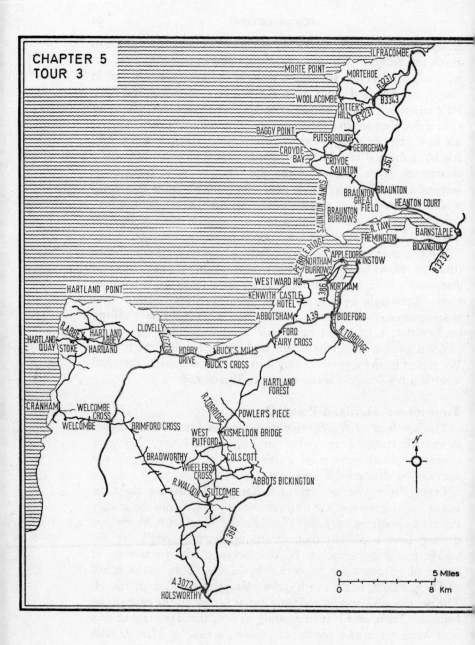

CHAPTER 5
TOUR 3

ILFRACOMBE
MORTE POINT
MORTEHOE
WOOLACOMBE
POTTER'S HILL
B3231
B3343
B3231
BAGGY POINT
PUTSBOROUGH
GEORGEHAM
CROYDE BAY
CROYDE
SAUNTON
A361
BRAUNTON GREAT FIELD
BRAUNTON
HEANTON COURT
BRAUNTON BURROWS
SAUNTON SANDS
R. TAW
FREMINGTON
BARNSTAPLE
BICKINGTON
PEBBLE RIDGE
APPLEDORE
NORTHAM BURROWS
INSTOW
B3232
WESTWARD HO!
NORTHAM
KENWITH CASTLE HOTEL
A386
ABBOTSHAM
A39
BIDEFORD
HARTLAND POINT
FORD
FAIRY CROSS
R. TORRIDGE
CLOVELLY
B3237
HOBBY DRIVE
BUCK'S MILLS
BUCK'S CROSS
HARTLAND ABBEY
HARTLAND QUAY
R. ABBEY
STOKE
HARTLAND
HARTLAND FOREST
CRANHAM
WELCOME CROSS
POWLER'S PIECE
R. TORRIDGE
WELCOME
BRIMFORD CROSS
WEST PUTFORD
KISMELDON BRIDGE
BRADWORTHY
COLSCOTT
WHEELERS CROSS
ABBOTS BICKINGTON
R. WALDON
SUTCOMBE
A388
N

A3072
HOLSWORTHY

0   5 Miles
0   8 Km

At Woolacombe we have to turn inland behind the dunes, but we remain as closely as possible to the coast by keeping right, soon climbing a 1 in 4 hill beside the green peak of Potters Hill. At a T-junction on the plateau turn right on the B3231 for Georgeham and Croyde. We drive through both these villages, which have pretty corners beside a stream, and at Croyde post office turn right for Croyde Bay and Putsborough, at the Croyde Bay turn going forward for Putsborough. This little detour of three-quarters of a mile is well worth doing, in spite of its steep climb and sharp bend, for Putsborough is an exceptionally charming group of thatched cottages and two-storey manor-house, seen to the left of the ford. We can turn by some newer houses built on the solid rock and retrace our way to Croyde, continuing through the village on the way to Saunton and Braunton on a fine cliff road from which we have one of the best views across Croyde Bay to Baggy Point. As we round the headland we have a magnificent panorama before us stretching over Saunton Sands and Braunton Burrows nature reserve to the mouth of the Taw.

Motorists studying the one-inch ordnance survey map of the district (No. 163) may be puzzled by the large area over a mile square marked 'Braunton Great Field'. This is the largest survival in England of the old Saxon strip system, when the agricultural land near the Saxon settlements was divided into strips and three separate strips were allotted to each member of the community to cultivate. This agricultural tradition is unbroken, though the land is now divided among only eight farmers. For a sight of this vast expanse turn right before reaching the centre of Braunton, just beyond some old cottages, where two turnings leave the main street at the same point, one marked Burrows Park and Close, the other Field Lane. Either of these will bring us to the edge of the Great Field.

At the town centre beyond the railway turn right for Barnstaple, shortly driving in sight of the estuary and later beside it for some distance. We pass the seventeenth-century Heanton Court, now a hotel, before entering the outskirts of Barnstaple. In the centre we join the A39 for Bideford, crossing the Taw, and driving through the villages of Bickington and Fremington to Instow, where we leave the Taw estuary and now drive beside that of the Torridge. At Instow keep right to the waterside road, looking across to Appledore, and thence our road follows the shore closely all the way to Bideford.

About half a mile beyond Instow we pass the iron gates and lodge of Tapeley Park, the beautiful gardens of which are open to the public daily (except Mondays and Saturdays) from June to mid-September. The imposing Georgian house was the home of John Christie, the founder of Glyndebourne.

Cross the Torridge into Bideford and keep right along the quayside on A386 for Northam, the home of the 'Potwallopers'. Many readers may have seen these doughty stalwarts in action on television programmes, but for those who have not it should be explained that the people of Northam have ancient grazing rights on Northam Burrows in return for maintaining the pebble ridge on the seaward side. The smooth round pebbles are constantly being shifted by the sea, and once a year the 'Potwallopers' throw the pebbles back to fill the gaps in the natural sea wall.

Turn right for Appledore in Northam and drive along to the harbour settlement, long famous for the boat building that is still an important industry. There are some pleasant Regency houses and Chanters Folly, a tower overlooking the estuary, was also built at the beginning of the nineteenth century, it is said by a ship-owner as a watch tower. We can continue past the church on the road signposted Westward Ho, looking down over Northam Burrows and the pebble ridge on our right. Bear left at a fork for Northam and after driving through the town turn right at the war memorial for Buckleigh. This is a high road with further splendid views across the burrows, and it brings us in a mile and a half to the sea at Westward Ho, a Victorian watering-place named after Charles Kingsley's famous novel. It is on record that Kingsley did not appreciate the honour and feared that this fine stretch of coast would be spoilt. (I wonder what he would think of it all today?) However, it has become a popular bathing resort and has ample car-parking space for the visitor.

Leave the town by the Abbotsham road, climbing a steep hill under trees, going on for Clovelly at a fork, and soon passing on our right Kenwith Castle Hotel, in sight of a tree-topped knoll where there is an earthwork, used in Saxon times, it is said, as a refuge from the Danes after they landed at Appledore late in the ninth century.

Beyond Abbotsham our road soon reaches A39, in which we

turn right for Clovelly. We pass through two little hamlets intriguingly named Ford and Fairy Cross, and in two and a half miles after the thatched Hoops inn we turn right at Buck's Cross for Buck's Mills, driving down a lush glen beside a stream to this tiny settlement with a nineteenth-century church, where there is a turning place and room for one or two cars just above the shore. A short walk will bring us to the sea, where we will find the remains of an old mill once powered by the stream that gushes down a shute, and can observe the interesting rock formations as we look along the coast.

On regaining the road to Clovelly drive straight there, noting on our right the entrance to the Hobby Drive and Gallantry Bower, which is open to cars for a moderate charge. Clovelly is world-famous and it hardly seems necessary to gild the lily, except to say thankfully that its picturesque cobbled street, lined with lovely cottages and traditionally negotiated by donkeys, happily remains unspoilt. We retrace our way towards the main road, but this time turn aside where Hartland is signposted on the right, in under half a mile turning right again. Continue on this minor road to a fork, where we take the right branch for Hartland Point and Lighthouse, leaving the village with Hartland church on the skyline to our left for the time being. There is a well-placed parking space just short of the signal station and lighthouse, which can both be visited and are interesting to grown-ups and children alike.

We return from the point as far as a signposted road to Stoke and Hartland Quay at the crossing of a stream, a single-track road but with adequate passing places. We soon begin to descend into a deep combe, its sides clad with many venerable oaks, and cross the Abbey river. The river's name and the Georgian Gothic Hartland Abbey are the sole reminders of the proud monastery of Austin canons which replaced an earlier foundation by King Harold's mother, and in turn disappeared. Beyond the river we soon enter the village of Stoke, where Hartland's church of St Nectan stands. This magnificant church has a tower which is a landmark for many miles and is said to be the highest in Devon and Cornwall. The church is entered between a short avenue of gnarled lime trees leading to the swinging lych gate, and beside the gate is a wide stile over which the restored memorial cross to St Nectan is seen.

The interior of the church is a treasure-house for the antiquarian, its spacious and lofty nave and chancel divided by a
sumptuous rood screen with carving of almost unbelievable rich-
ness, while the embellished ceiling of the little chapel of St Mary's
Guild is a perfect gem. The font is a particularly beautiful example of Late Norman craftsmanship, highly ornamented with
arcading, scallops and zigzag moulding. Interesting monuments
are among the many other features to detain even the layman
from continuing his travels until he has seen all.

Reluctantly we return down the little path between the limes,
noting the picturesque cottages beside it which were formerly the
church house, and leave the village by the road signposted
Hartland Quay, a short mile away. The little quay, once so
important that the hotel incorporated a bank which issued its
own £1 and £5 notes (one can be seen in the hotel at the present
day), is now fallen into disuse, but it is the only place accessible
by motor road where the fantastic cliffs of this stretch of coast
can be seen at close quarters, the strata weirdly contorted by the
folding of the rocks comparatively early in geological time, while
savage rocks like the well-named Shark's Fins reach out to
menace approaching ships. Unfortunately we can only see on
foot the high waterfalls dashing over the cliffs at intervals along
the coast where streams have not yet worn a channel for themselves at a lower level.

To resume our route we must return to Hartland church and
turn right for Welcombe a few yards beyond it, thereafter
following the signposts to Welcombe, after about four miles
turning left beyond Cranham and crossing a stream for Welcombe
church. This little church is also dedicated to St Nectan and has
one of the earliest timber screens in Devon, and on the opposite
side of the road is one of the numerous holy wells found in this
part of the country. Continue past the church on the same road
for almost two and a half miles towards Bideford and at Welcombe
Cross on A39 go forward for Bradworthy, right at the next
junction, and right again at Brimford Cross along an unsignposted road. In a mile and a quarter go forward once more for
Bradworthy, but at the subsequent staggered crossroads leave
the Bradworthy road, turning right for Holsworthy, which is
reached after seven miles over pleasant hill country, mainly
pastoral, with no special highlights.

St Michael's Mount. (Chapter 7.)

Entrance to Caerhays Castle. (Chapter 7.)

Mevagissey harbour. (Chapter 7.)

Manaccan, cottage with typical coloured glass porch. (Chapter 7.)

Holsworthy is a high-set market town with a pleasant central market place and a medieval church with a tall Perpendicular tower on the eastern outskirts of the town. Here we take the Bideford road, A388, turning left at a telephone box just before leaving the built-up area, then right in a few yards, both turnings currently unsignposted. From that point we have nearly three miles of straightforward driving before we turn right at a T-junction for Sutcombe, left at the next junction, and right at a subsequent unsignposted T-junction. In half a mile we turn left at a crossroads and are soon dipping down to cross a tiny stream before crossing the bridge over the river Waldon into Sutcombe.

We drive through the village on the Bradworthy road, after a mile turning right for Abbots Bickington, but turn left again towards Bradworthy at the next crossroads. We are now making for Bideford, and turn right for West Putford, then turn left at the next two junctions for Bideford, forward at Churston, then soon cross the Torridge and follow the signposts to Bideford. At Powler's Piece crossroads we enter Hartland Forest and drive through its dense woodlands and past the reservoir near its outskirts, then follow the fine wooded valley of a tributary to its junction with the river Yeo. Our road again runs near the bank of the river and it is a lovely ride to the junction with the main road, A386, in about three miles, and so back to Bideford, Barnstaple and Ilfracombe by the old road route, as for the first tour in this chapter.

D.C.—6

EAST AND WEST OF THE TAMAR

THE TOURS in this chapter range from the South Hams and the south-western edge of Dartmoor to the grand coastline of Cornwall as far as the Fowey river. Plymouth is the natural centre of all this country, in a commanding position on the Sound, into which flows four great rivers, the Tamar, the Tavy, the Plym and the Lynher. It is hardly necessary to stress Plymouth's fame, both ancient and modern, and there are so many links with its historic past that a day is needed to explore it even cursorily.

We can park on the water front under the Hoe and from there are within reach of the statue of Sir Francis Drake (Mayor of Plymouth in 1582), looking across to the island named after him, and near him Smeaton's Eddystone lighthouse and the Naval War Memorial. To the east is the Royal Citadel, built during King Charles II's reign, entered by an elaborate gateway, and below are Sutton Harbour and the Mayflower Steps (marked by a plain arch on Doric columns), and the old part of Plymouth known as the Barbican. Here there are many ancient Elizabethan houses, one of which (32 New Street) is open to the public on weekdays, and on Sundays also in the summer months. Here, too, we shall find a link with very recent times, the renamed Sir Francis Chichester inn. This does not begin to exhaust Plymouth's interest, and in addition there are the Royal Naval Dockyard, the barracks and other important buildings at Devonport, and the Royal Naval Hospital and the Royal Marine Barracks at Stonehouse.

Tour one: Tavistock, South-west Dartmoor

The first tour, of about ninety miles, after crossing the Tamar, takes in some of the dramatic scenery around Tavistock and on south-western Dartmoor. It can be followed just as conveniently from Tavistock as from Plymouth, as well as from other places on

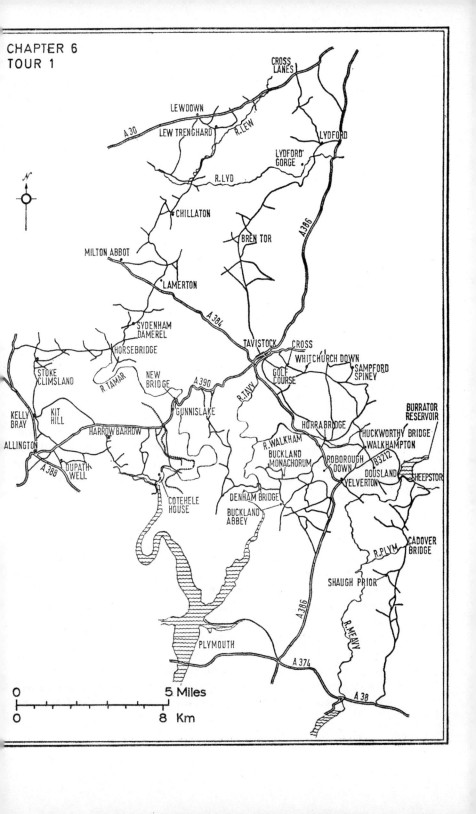

CHAPTER 6
TOUR 1

N

CROSS LANES
LEWDOWN
LEW TRENCHARD
R. LEW
A 30
LYDFORD
LYDFORD GORGE
R. LYD
A 386
CHILLATON
BREN TOR
MILTON ABBOT
LAMERTON
A 384
SYDENHAM DAMEREL
TAVISTOCK
CROSS
HORSEBRIDGE
WHITCHURCH DOWN
SAMPFORD SPINEY
STOKE CLIMSLAND
NEW BRIDGE
A 390
GOLF COURSE
R. TAMAR
R. TAVY
BURRATOR RESERVOIR
KELLY BRAY
KIT HILL
GUNNISLAKE
HORRABRIDGE
HUCKWORTHY BRIDGE
HARROW BARROW
R. WALKHAM
WALKHAMPTON
ALLINGTON
A 388
DUPATH WELL
BUCKLAND MONACHORUM
ROBOROUGH DOWN
B 3212
DOUSLAND
SHEEPSTOR
VELVERTON
COTEHELE HOUSE
DENHAM BRIDGE
BUCKLAND ABBEY
CADOVER BRIDGE
R. PLYM
R. PLYM
SHAUGH PRIOR
A 386
R. MEAVY
PLYMOUTH
A 374
A 38

0   5 Miles
0   8 Km

the route, and from Yelverton, only four miles from Tavistock. We leave Plymouth by the Tavistock road (A386) and turn left for Bere Alston just after a crossroads on Roborough Down (about six miles from Plymouth's centre). The views are superb from this high road, especially to the looming western slopes of Dartmoor on our right. We follow the minor road (neglecting side turnings) until it brings us to the entrance to Buckland Abbey, the famous home of Sir Francis Drake on the site of a Cistercian monastery, parts of which are incorporated in the Tudor mansion. Drake's drum and other relics are shown to visitors, who are admitted on weekdays and Sunday afternoons from Easter to the end of September, and at other times of the year on Wednesday, Saturday and Sunday afternoons. The abbey tithe barn houses a collection of old vehicles.

On leaving the gates of the lovely park turn sharp left for Buckland Monachorum and in a mile come to the outskirts of the village at a T-junction, where we turn right and then left. (The Garden House, with fine landscaped gardens open on Wednesday afternoons from April to September, is half a mile along the Tavistock road.) The imposing church of Buckland is a fine Perpendicular structure with a high pinnacled tower and its link with Drake is confirmed by the south chapel built by him when he lived at the Abbey. In addition to the font which is contemporary with the church there is a Saxon tub font, discovered during repairs to the foundations, which suggests the existence of an earlier church on the site. There are some ancient stone cottages in the village and the school beside the church was endowed in 1702 by Lady Modyford, as its inscription states.

We retrace our way past the shuttered Drake Manor inn to the second T-junction and there go forward for Green Lane, descending into the magnificent wooded valley of the Tavy to cross the river at Denham bridge, an ancient high arch spanning a deep gorge. A steep hairpin bend on the way down needs careful negotiation, and on the other side of the bridge there is a 1 in 4 hill to climb through the dense woods rising above the river. At the top turn right for Tavistock, and again right on a major road, then bear to the left at a wide junction. At a crossroads by a handsome stone house go forward on the Milton Abbot road, turning left at the next crossroads away from Tavistock and

dropping steeply down towards the twisting Tamar valley, to
which we now aim on the main road, the A390, to cross the river
by the 'New Bridge', a fine granite fourteenth-century bridge.
From the valley we ascend the long hill to Gunnislake and turn
left beyond it for Cotehele, which is reliably signposted at all
subsequent junctions.

This beautiful old stone house, built mainly in the fifteenth and
sixteenth centuries, was the home of the Edgcumbe family before
their removal to Mount Edgcumbe. The walls of the lofty
Great Hall are hung with armour and weapons, and other rooms
contain furniture and tapestries which have been in the house
since they were acquired. The house is open daily, except
Mondays, from April to September, and in the other months on
Wednesday, Saturday and Sunday afternoons. After seeing the
house we continue through the beautiful woods down to the quay
on the Tamar, a peaceful spot where there is a car park, and from
there turn left to cross an old stone bridge over a tributary stream.
We are still in the midst of luxuriant woodland as we keep closely
beside the stream for well over a mile, then turn right to cross it
and go on for Harrowbarrow, where we turn left for Callington
and at the main road left again for a few yards to the signposted
turning for Dupath Well, which after a second left turn is along
a little track leading from farm buildings. This is one of the best
holy wells in the country, believed to date from the fifteenth
century. The little chapel is built entirely of granite, even the
roof being composed of long granite slabs, and crowned with a
little pinnacled turret and pinnacles at each corner, the whole of
primitive workmanship. The pure spring water runs into the
baptismal bath as it has done from the time it was bulit.

We resume our route at the main road, turning right towards
Tavistock and in under a quarter of a mile left for Kelly Bray,
driving round the foot of Kit Hill (1,091 ft), surmounted by an
old mine chimney, as well as a less obvious prehistoric camp. At
Kelly Bray turn right on the Launceston road, then go straight on
for Stoke Climsland where the main road bears left. The road
goes straight through to Stoke Climsland in about a mile and a
half and continues past the church. At the crossroads above the
village turn right and follow this road to Horse Bridge, another
fine medieval bridge of seven arches by which we recross the
Tamar into Devon. On the Devon side of the river turn left,

then fork right by a house just beyond the Royal inn towards Lamerton, shortly forking left for Sydenham Damarel.

At a crossroads beyond the latter village turn right for Tavistock, driving through a wooded combe and up to another crossroads, then cross the main road (A384) for Chillaton. Thereafter follow the signposts to Chillaton, keeping left at a slate-hung toll house, and in the village go straight on past the gay Chichester Arms towards Lewdown. Thereafter we make for Lewdown, which is reliably signposted at each junction, soon going through the fine woodlands of the Lew valley. In about three miles, shortly after crossing the river, we pass the little church in the woods of Lew Trenchard and nearby Lew House, the seventeenth-century home of the Rev. S. Baring-Gould, the author and ecclesiastical expert who was rector here for over fifty years. There are a number of monuments to members of the family in the church.

After this we soon reach the main road, the A30, at Lewdown, where we turn right towards Okehampton and follow this road above the Lew valley for just over three miles to Cross Lanes, a minor crossroad, where we turn right for Lydford up a little lane which takes us directly to Lydford in less than three miles over well-wooded country. In Lydford turn right at the major road for Lydford Gorge, passing the square Norman keep of Lydford Castle on a high mound, and near it the ancient church dedicated to St Petrock, the sixth-century Celtic saint. At the bridge over the Lyd gorge there is a small car park, and from it there is a footpath through the gorge, in the care of the National Trust, and this may be followed in the summer months on payment of a small fee. It is a lovely walk, with two fine cascades, but is really for the adventurous and sure-footed, for the path is difficult in places.

Now we continue to Brentor, where we shall find another exciting feature, the volcanic peak crowned by the Church of St Michael, a medieval church with a battlemented tower which we soon see ahead of us. There is a car park opposite the gate to the church, which is well worth the climb not only to see the interior but to admire the spectacular views of Dartmoor and Lydford Gorge from the summit. Outcrops of pumice from the extinct volcano may be seen on the way up.

We continue past Brentor to Tavistock along a pleasant road

and reach the town in under four miles. Tavistock is a fine town, a worthy successor to the great abbey and market town that preceded it. After the abbey was given to the Earl of Bedford at the dissolution he and his successors were responsible for many impressive buildings in and near the centre. Fragments of the abbey survive near the Georgian Bedford Hotel, including the chapel beside the hotel, which was the frater. There are many manorial houses of the nineteenth century, evidence of the interest the Dukes of Bedford took in their tenants. The handsome fifteenth-century church stands near the site of the old abbey church. The Drake statue, a duplicate of the one on Plymouth Hoe, is a reminder that the great sailor was born in the parish.

From the centre cross the river Tavy and bear right (away from Princetown) and shortly turn left up Down road and on emerging to an open view over Whitchurch Down turn left, then right by an old cross of primitive workmanship, our road going over the golf course. At all subsequent crossroads and junctions continue for Sampford Spiney and later Sampford church, looking to the high tors of western Dartmoor. After the church drive on along a beech-lined road and bear right for Horrabridge. We pass another old cross on our right, then at the next crossroads turn left for Walkhampton, descending a steep hill to cross the river Walkham, flowing along a rocky bed, at Huckworthy Bridge. At Walkhampton go forward at the war memorial for Dousland and there cross a major road, the B3212, by an hotel, where Sheepstor is signposted. At the next junction bear left over the open moor, overlooking the densely wooded valley of the Meavy before we come to the gigantic dam across the river which has created the Burrator Reservoir.

This beautiful artificial lake supplies Plymouth with water and endorses the wisdom and skill of Sir Francis Drake, who brought Plymouth its first water supply from the same source. After a careful survey, he constructed a leat from Burrator Falls, and the water was flowing into Plymouth in April 1591, only a few months after the work began in December 1590. Modern engineers could not better his site or his speed! This remarkable achievement is commemorated every year on a June Saturday by a ceremony at which the Lord Mayor and members of the City Council inspect the water works at Burrator and drink a toast to

Sir Francis Drake, this being followed by a 'Fishing Feast' served in a marquee beside the reservoir.

Drive round the wooded shore of the lake and enjoy the many fine vistas across it, but instead of going back to the dam turn left into Sheepstor at the junction near the village. This little village has several interesting features. It is easiest to leave the car by the old cross outside the church, as our next turning is opposite, and see the church interior and in the churchyard the graves of the first Rajah Brooke and his successor, then go on past the old church house (dated 1658) to see the ancient Gothic St Leonard's Well by the roadside. We now take the little road opposite the cross, go over a stream, and climb over the moor, reaching nearly 900 ft, where the extensive views reward our courage in starting off in such a tiny lane. At a т-junction turn left, then continue to Cadover Bridge, where we cross the river Plym, once in a pleasant setting but now rather marred by the china clay workings of Lee Moor. From here we return to Plymouth via Shaugh Prior (just off the road) and Plympton, whose traditions go back further than those of Plymouth. It grew up round a priory and castle and the fine houses on columns and arcaded guildhall, as well as its medieval church, bear witness to its importance.

Tour two: Salcombe, South Hams

The second tour, of little over 110 miles, follows the coast east to Salcombe and crosses the fertile landscapes of the South Hams. We leave Plymouth by the Plymstock road (A379) and turn right at the crossroads where Saltram House is signposted to the left. This outstandingly beautiful Georgian house with rooms designed by Robert Adam should be noted for a visit at another time. It is open in the afternoon daily (except Tuesdays) from April to September. Follow the signposts to Hooe, turning right at the end of Radford Park Road and down into a wooded dip. A quarter of a mile after crossing a stream we take the first turning to the left beside a row of cottages, passing a handsome Georgian house on our right as we proceed uphill. Bear left at the next junction halfway up the hill, then at the top turn right for Bovisand and in less than half a mile turn left into a wooded valley which runs down to the sea. At the foot there is a parking space by the sea but there is now no through way, so we must return up the valley and turn right at the junction and then go forward for Staddiscombe. At the village bear left at an unsignposted junction and go right-handed through it, going right and forward for Down Thomas. At a later junction turn right again for Down Thomas, and in that village turn left for Heybrook Bay

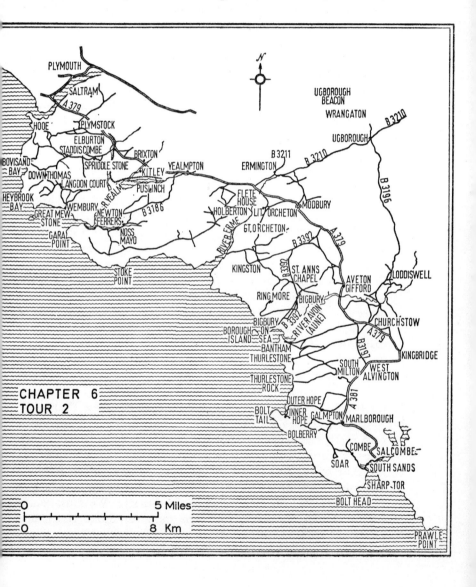

CHAPTER 6
TOUR 2

0   5 Miles

0   8 Km

and thence follow the signposts to the bay, where there is a splendid sea and coast view, with the Great Mew Stone out to sea.

Return to Down Thomas and turn right for Gabber, left at a T-junction for Elburton, then right for Wembury Beach, passing the entrance to Langdon Court, now a hotel, and looking across to Gara Point before we descend through woods to the beach. After crossing the stream at the foot of the combe turn right along a narrow lane below the church, high on the cliff facing out to sea, to bring us to a well-positioned car park on the cliff, from where there are cliff paths in both directions. From the car park return past the church to the junction and there go forward up Church Road and turn right where Elburton is signposted in about three-quarters of a mile, then left by the Jubilee inn. At the next T-junction turn left towards Plymstock, in another half mile turning right for Spriddlestone and Brixton, this latter road eventually bringing us to the main road, where we turn right along the way surprisingly signposted Totnes.

After driving through Brixton we skirt the beautiful park of Kitley estate. According to tradition the famous nursery rhyme of 'Old Mother Hubbard' was written at Kitley House and the picturesque thatched cottage in Yealmpton, half a mile from the park on the main road, is known as Mother Hubbard's Cottage. We do not go as far as Yealmpton but turn right at the end of the estate for Newton Ferrers and Noss Mayo, descending to cross a causeway and bridge over the river Yealm. As we climb out of the valley we pass on our right the splendid early Georgian mansion of Puslinch, in mellow brick with stone facings. Now we continue to Newton Ferrers, turning right at a T-junction, and in the village drive on past the medieval church on the lower road as far as the turning place to see the yacht moorings and the beautiful wooded slopes above the estuary of the Yealm.

We return through the village to the church and beyond it turn right, round the head of the creek into Noss Mayo, which faces its sister village of Newton Ferrers across the water. At the church we drive down to the creek, where we can follow a waterside road through dense woodlands for nearly a mile to a turning place for further views of the estuary. We must return to the church, however, and turn right for Stoke Beach and Holbeton, turning left at Stoke Cross to Holbeton along a high-level road parallel with the sea but only catching occasional glimpses through gates and gaps in the hedges. The road later veers inland as we approach Holbeton and we make for the church in the centre, turning left past the Mildmay Colours inn, and leave the church on our left as we go forward, winding our way steeply down to cross a little stream by thatched cottages. On the ascent fork left for Yealmpton and turn right at the next T-junction, a few yards farther turning right on the main road towards Modbury by the entrance to Flete House, an Elizabethan manor-house which is open to visitors on Wednesday and Thursday afternoons from May to September. A mile and a half from here, after crossing the river Erme, turn right for Orcheton and Kingston into a little road which takes us along a winding course to Kingston with several ups and downs, passing Little Orcheton and Great Orcheton farms on the way.

We enter the village by the beautiful old thatched forge, where we go forward, and after nearly two miles, just short of a major road, turn right for Ringmore for a detour to one of the most attractive villages in this part of Devon. We come to the church in under a mile and from there can make a little circuit of the village and see its beautiful thatched cottages and thirteenth-century Journey's End inn, preferably on foot, though it is possible to drive round, with only one rocky stretch of road down to the inn. The church is an interesting one, also of the thirteenth century, with a tower on the south side, the lower part doing duty as a porch.

After returning to the junction go forward to the major road past the Pickwick inn at St Ann's Chapel and turn right to Bigbury, going on through the village to Bigbury-on-Sea, where there are magnificent views over Bigbury Bay to Bolt Tail and Stoke Point and a grand beach which can be crossed at low tide to Borough Island. Ample car parks are provided near the beach. To resume our way we return to Bigbury village and turn left towards Modbury and at the next crossroads right for Aveton Gifford, in about a mile and a quarter turning right on the main road to the village. The church, up a little road to the left, was unfortunately one that suffered from the bombing of the second world war, though it has now been rebuilt. At the far end of the village cross the long causeway and bridge over the Aune and follow the road towards Salcombe for another mile, then turn right for Bantham at the signposted crossroads.

After two miles we descend steadily from the plateau into the village and drive past the Sloop inn and a row of charming thatched cottages to a large car park behind the sand dunes at the mouth of the Aune (this spelling is the Devon version of Avon). The river winds to the sea round the Ham, below which there are a few houses tucked in, completely sheltered, and swans are usually to be seen on the estuary.

Returning to the village, fork right beyond the Sloop inn and right downhill at a small hamlet, then right at a T-junction up a steep hill, soon turning right into Thurlestone, another picturesque village of thatched cottages and hydrangea-filled gardens. The beautiful garden of the Old Rectory on the left is open daily from April to the end of September, and the view along the coast from the garden is superb. We continue past the church, noting the ancient cross outside, and on to the car park beyond the golf course, from where we look across the beach to the Thurlestone, a natural rock arch. From here we continue to the village of South Milton, where the church of All Saints has fine screens and a curious early Norman font with heads and animals, the moulding so thick and primitive that it looks like a child's efforts in plasticine.

We drive on through the village, again mainly of thatched cottages, on the Salcombe road and at the main road turn right, leaving it in a long half mile for Galmpton and Hope Cove, passing through the former village on the way down to the cove under the high promontory of Bolt Tail. We leave Hope, which has become popular as a resort in recent times, for Inner Hope and Bolberry, turning right at a T-junction at Bolberry Cross for Soar, and right again at the next T-junction. Three-quarters of a mile beyond this junction turn left for Combe and South Sands, at Combe turning down the wooded valley to the sandy cove, with views to Prawle Point. The road forward from the junction leads to Sharpitor, a garden behind Bolt Head giving magnificent views, and the Overbecks Museum in the house. The garden is open daily all through the year, and the museum from March to October, except on Saturdays.

At the other end of South Sands cove we drive up a steep hill to reach North Sands, an equally lovely cove with a commodious car park behind the sands. Now continue uphill into Salcombe, keeping to the cliff road to obtain views across the estuary. King

Henry VIII's castle is below us beside the water, one of the series of defensive fortifications in south Devon, best seen from our previous road to South Sands. Salcombe has developed as a holiday and yachting resort and the town is now quite extensive. We encircle it, following the one-way system, and climb up a steep road away from the water front with views through luxuriant hanging woods to the estuary and coves on the opposite shore. Joining A381, we soon leave the town behind, and continue through Malborough towards West Alvington, still on a high road giving long views to the right. We turn off the main road before West Alvington on to the B3197, however, forking left for Modbury one and a quarter miles short of Kingsbridge and after a long mile turn right at a crossroads for Churchstow, originally the mother parish of Kingsbridge. The tall grey tower of the church is typical of those in the South Hams, and the Church House inn opposite the entrance, dated 1250, claims to have been a Benedictine Monks' rest house.

In another half mile on the A379 fork left on to the B3194 for Loddiswell, and again go left by a prominent clump of trees at a crossroads, soon descending to cross the river Aune (or Avon) in its deep wooded valley, and climbing out of the valley to the hillside village of Loddiswell, looking down to the church on our right. From here go forward for Wrangaton, on the B3196, steering towards the southerly slopes of Dartmoor and soon see Ugborough Beacon silhouetted against the sky before we join B3210 and turn left towards Plymouth. We leave this road temporarily for a short detour (right) into Ugborough's spacious central square, where the majestic church stands in a commanding position on the south side. The beautiful tower is almost 100 ft high while, inside, the fine stone pulpit and carved and painted screens are of the fifteenth century, and there is a brass of a sixteenth-century lady.

We turn left at the bottom of Ugborough's square to rejoin the Ermington road and after just over two miles turn left for Modbury. This is a delightful little town with a main street of gracious Georgian and earlier houses, among which is set the exquisite half-timbered and gabled Exeter inn, dating from at least as early as the sixteenth century. The White Hart and incorporated Assembly Room is a pleasing essay in the Georgian style, while the early nineteenth-century Traine House has a colonnade, and opposite this is the grandiose pinnacled conduit dating from the beginning of the eighteenth century. The feeling of stepping back into the past is very insistent in the peaceful atmosphere. The church, away from the main part of the town, is remarkable for its tower, which tapers from the ground by stages and ends in a slender spire.

We retrace our way back from the town to the top of the hill and bear left at each junction for Ermington, crossing the Erme into the village, memorable to most people for its bent spire. We continue beyond the village until we reach the main road, A379, turning right for Plymouth, via Yealmpton. On the left as we enter the latter we pass Old Mother Hubbard's Cottage, referred to earlier in the tour, and later the nineteenth-century church, and so back to Plymouth through Brixton, Plymstock, and Laira Bridge.

Tour three: Rame, Polperro, St Germans

The last tour from Plymouth goes via Torpoint Ferry along the rugged coast of Cornwall beyond Polperro and covers about ninety miles. Take the Torpoint Ferry across the Hamoaze and on landing follow A374 through the built-up area of Torpoint, soon emerging into open country with one of the best views to Saltash bridge on our right. We soon pass the entrance to Antony House, a beautiful Queen Anne house containing many family portraits of the Carew family as well as good furniture, usually open to visitors though unfortunately closed for repairs in 1969. The house is set in a landscaped park from which there are views across the Lynher and down towards the mouth where the river flows into the Hamoaze.

Antony village is some distance from the house (almost two miles) and when we enter it we keep left at the fork and turn left beyond the Ring o' Bells inn for St John, where we go forward past the church, which retains its squat Norman tower with a pyramid cap. Millbrook, the next village we come to, is a larger one of less ancient appearance. Turn right into it and after passing the church on the right turn left twice at crossroads for Millbrook Quay to drive round the waterside road along the shore of Millbrook Lake. High wooded slopes rise to our right and we soon look across the Hamoaze to Devonport. After a mile and a half the road climbs away from the waterside to a

T-junction, where we turn left, and brings us along the boundary
of Mount Edgcumbe Park to Stonehouse passenger ferry. Near
the ferry a castellated lodge stands beside the entrance to Mount
Edgcumbe, and from this point we have a clear view to the
embowered house, rebuilt on the former plan after its destruction
in the second world war.

We return alongside the lovely park to the T-junction, there
going forward through woods, and at the end of the Mount
Edgcumbe estate Maker church stands in complete isolation on
the highest point. The south aisle of the church was built as a
chapel for the Edgcumbes and there are several monuments to
members of the family. Maker school is a mile beyond the church
and here we bear left for Cawsand and are soon looking over
Cawsand Bay to the wooded promontory on the south ending
at Penlee Point. At the next junction turn left to Kingsand, a
fishing village of tiny streets and colour-washed cottages along
the shore which earned its proud prefix on account of the
landing here of King Henry VII. Kingsand and Cawsand are
contiguous and we cannot really distinguish the point where we

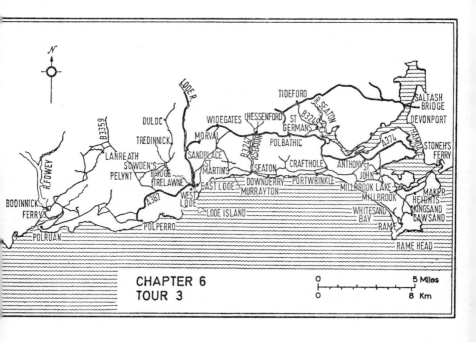

CHAPTER 6
TOUR 3

leave one and enter the other, but the Smuggler's inn in Cawsand's square recalls old legends of smuggling in both villages.

Continue from Cawsand steeply uphill and go forward for Rame, keeping left at a junction for Rame Head and church, which is the nearest practicable point to Rame Head, though a road leads from there to the coastguards station, from which a footpath leads to the headland. From the church we return to the farm at the junction and turn left just beyond it along an unsignposted lane which emerges as a grand cliff road giving splendid views along Whitesand Bay and soon retrospectively to Rame Head, surmounted by a ruined chapel. Far out to sea the lighthouse on the treacherous Eddystone rocks may be sighted on a clear day.

After several miles along this splendid road, one of the best cliff roads in the south-west, turn inland slightly to join a major road, the B3247, turning left along it as far as Crafthole and beyond its centre turn left by a simple Celtic cross for Portwrinkle. As we drive down to shore level we look along the coast to Looe Island, and from the spacious parking space above the beach we look back to Rame Head.

Resuming our way along the coast at the crossroads, we turn left after two miles for Downderry to keep to the high cliff road then descend to the attractive modern residential village, stretching for more than a mile, after which we drop down to cross the Seaton river, where another modern resort has grown up round the beach at the river's mouth. From here turn left along a minor road lined with pine trees which is signposted to Murrayton, and at a signposted junction turn right for Looe. A small lane leads off this road to the left to the Monkey Sanctuary at Murrayton, which animal lovers may care to visit.

On our way to Looe we join a major road, the B3253, above a wooded valley and pass St Martin's, the mother church of East Looe, which faces its sister town, West Looe, across the Looe river. Both have become popular holiday resorts. East Looe has some narrow streets of old houses and retains in the High Street the old Guildhall with outside stairs under its gabled porch. We cross to West Looe by the bridge, from which we can look up the wooded Looe valley as well as at East and West Looe from below, both pleasing compositions building up from the waterside. From West Looe the most convenient way to Polperro is along the main road leading up from the end of the bridge, which as it

Old cottages in Boscastle
village   (Chapter 8.)

Bodinnick ferry, Fowey
river.   (Chapter 7.)

Cliffs, Boscastle bay. (Chapter 8.)

Port Isaac. (Chapter 8.)

climbs to a high point gives a view on the right of the meeting of the two densely wooded valleys of the Looe and West Looe rivers.

Polperro has some claim to be described as one of the loveliest villages on the Cornish coast, and the picturesque streets and quaint corners are even narrower and more difficult to negotiate than most encountered in ancient settlements. It is, therefore, obligatory in the season to leave the car at the ample car park at the top of the town and explore on foot. This is no great hardship, for few can visit Polperro without falling under the spell of its charm and atmosphere. Among the many old houses the house of Dr Jonathan Couch, grandfather of Sir Arthur Quiller-Couch, and the Buccaneer's Rest, decorated with carved faces, are noteworthy.

On leaving the car park turn right on the road signposted Bodinnick and Polruan, which are signposted at each junction, and where the road divides keep left for Polruan, turning right at a later T-junction. At Polruan we cannot do better than follow the signs to 'official car park overlooking harbour' for this is a wonderful viewpoint at the top of St Saviour's Hill high above the Fowey estuary and looking across it to Fowey. From here we must retrace our way to the parting of the ways and now take the road to Bodinnick, and on arriving at the village fork left for the car ferry, which crosses to Fowey. This time we are not taking the ferry but continue forward and uphill, looking across to the wooded banks on the farther shore of the estuary (marred a little by the china clay railway and quays).

Lanreath is our next destination and we go forward over a low plateau divided into mainly pasture fields, but interspersed with some ploughed fields, for over four miles, turning right into the village. By the attractive Punchbowl inn and restaurant facing the church we turn left for Pelynt and at a major road, the B3359, right towards Polperro, this latter road taking us through Pelynt and on for more than a mile before we turn left for Sowden's Bridge, shortly passing the entrance to Trelawne, the home of Bishop Trelawney, one of the famous Seven Bishops who were put on trial by King James II for refusing to accept the Declaration of Indulgence, and acquitted. Beyond this we descend into a richly wooded combe, turning left when it joins the equally wooded valley of the West Looe river, which we cross at Sowden's Bridge on the road to Duloe, climbing out of the valley up a

D.C.—7

narrow twisting road which bears left at a junction with three
lanes to the right.

After passing through the little cottage group of Tredinnick we
come to a major road, the B3254, where we turn right for Sand-
place, which lies at the point where we cross the Looe river and
the railway. A short distance beyond the crossing we turn left
on to the main road, the A387, for Torpoint and follow this road
over well-wooded country through Morval, Widegates and
Hessenford, where we cross the river Seaton, to St Germans,
turning left off the A38 at Polbathic in sight of a tidal creek.

St Germans is one of the most historic places in Cornwall. In
the first place, it takes its name from the Roman St Germanus,
who came to England to spread Christianity in the early part of
the fifth century, but there is no evidence of a church on the site
until the tenth century, when a Saxon church was built as the
cathedral of a bishopric and St Germans became the ecclesiastical
capital of Cornwall. When the see was removed to Crediton the
present beautiful Norman church was built as the priory church
of the Augustinian monastery which had taken the place of the
bishopric. The gabled west front, flanked by an octagonal tower
and a square one, has a beautiful Norman doorway with seven
richly decorated recessed arches, and inside the church massive
Norman piers support the nave arches on the south side. A fine
monument by Rysbrack commemorates Edward Eliot, in Roman
dress, who died in 1722, one of the family whose fine house stands
beside the church and incorporates what remained of the priory
buildings in the eighteenth century.

After leaving the church go forward through the village, near
its end passing the unusual Eliot almshouses, six seventeenth-
century houses with projecting gables over a balcony with outside
steps leading to it. We now continue back to Plymouth, reaching
the main road at Tideford, and thence over the splendid Saltash
bridge, the pride of Plymouth and Cornwall, which has in modern
times taken the place of the ancient ferry dating back to the
granting of its licence by the Black Prince, with an unbroken
record of service over the intervening six hundred years.

SOUTH CORNWALL

CORNWALL means to most holiday-makers a county of rocky coves and stretches of golden sands, and indeed the coastline is the great scenic attraction of Cornwall. Nevertheless exploration of the hinterland is rewarding too and the tours in this chapter combine the two aspects, visiting the highlights of the coast and the quieter inland scene, the typical villages and the many links with the past, going back as far as prehistoric times.

There are many good centres, even the smallest fishing village providing accommodation for the tourist, and it is possible to join the tours from all of them, as well as from the larger resorts, such as Falmouth and Truro, both originally old towns. Falmouth was important because of its position on a large and safe harbour and Pendennis Castle (open daily) is a link with the sixteenth century when such harbours needed to be defended. Now it is used by pleasure craft as much as by commercial shipping, and trips may be made up the Fal. Truro lies in an important position on the Truro river and is a fine town, though with a later appearance, partly because its imposing cathedral is mainly of the nineteenth century, only the south aisle remaining from the early parish church. The tall column crowned by a statue at the top of Lemon Street is a landmark, and is a memorial to Richard Lander, an African explorer born in the town in 1804.

Tour one: Roseland, Fowey

On the first tour, covering about 120 miles, we cross the King Harry Ferry and follow the coast as far as Fowey after exploring the Roseland peninsula, so that we can start from Truro on the A39, turning left to the ferry, or from Falmouth and Penryn we take the Truro road as far as the King Harry Ferry turn, which is on the right about a mile after Carnon Downs (B3289), turning left at a crossroads after a mile, and noting on the right the entrance to Trelissick gardens, which are open on weekdays and

Sunday afternoons from March to October. These lovely gardens with their many varieties of trees and shrubs, and parkland stretching to the shore of the river Fal, deserve a leisurable visit, so we will undoubtedly decide to leave them for a future occasion.

After passing a second entrance to the gardens we descend steeply to the ferry across the Fal, here flowing between densely wooded slopes, and drive up through the woods on the other side.

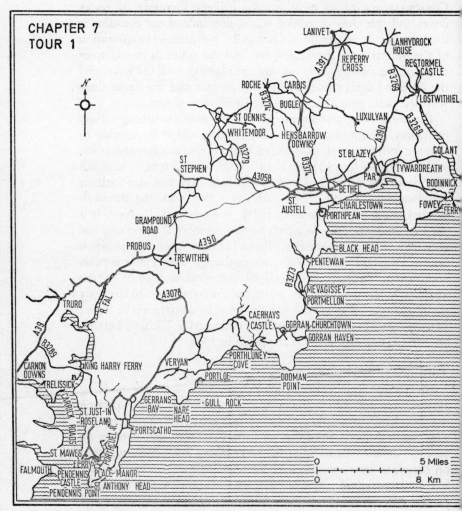

CHAPTER 7
TOUR 1

We are now in the romantic-sounding Roseland and soon after emerging from the woods we turn right for St Mawes, in two miles coming to St Just-in-Roseland, where we join the main road, the A3078. As we approach St Mawes we choose the left fork of the the two ways into St Mawes, bringing us to the east end of the waterfront town beloved by yachtsmen, looking across St Mawes harbour to the castle. We can drive right along the waterfront, one of the most attractive in Cornwall, looking across to the busy port of Falmouth. We pass the clover-shaped castle built in the reign of Henry VIII for the purposes of coastal defence, open to visitors daily. At this point we turn inland and continue as far as the junction with the ferry road, where we turn left along a lane signposted St Just Church. This is a wonderful road, lined with hydrangeas for much of the way and giving grand views of the creeks and promontories along Carrick Roads, and it brings us to the lych gate which has the effect of framing the church below. The tower has a square stair turret rising higher than its battlements, with a clock on the west face.

On returning to the main road take the right fork and cross the head of a wooded creek of the Porthcuel river, and passing an 'access only' road at the top of the ensuing hill continue to a signposted road to Gerrans, Anthony and Porthscatho. Porthscatho is signposted on the left before we reach Gerrans and we follow this road into the fishing village and in recent times holiday resort, from the harbour of which we have fine views across Gerrans Bay to Nare Point and its offshore Gull Rock, and beyond to Dodman Point.

From Porthscatho drive into Gerrans, reaching the village at the church, crowned by a tapering spire, and turning left for a detour to St Anthony up an avenue of ivy-clad trees forming a tunnel which veers left at the Country Club gate and descends to cross the head of a creek before reaching Place Manor and church beside the passenger ferry to St Mawes, where we look across the harbour. We retrace our way to the turning for St Anthony Head, from which there are even more splendid vistas up Carrick Roads, with Falmouth and Pendennis Castle prominent in the foreground. There is a car park on the headland to give us time to admire the scene, and on returning from this point we have a sea view on both sides of the road.

This time we drive right through Gerrans village to the main road, where we turn right and continue until we reach in about two miles a minor road on the right to Veryan. A mile along this road is the truly beautiful village of Veryan, set in a bower of trees with the church near the centre behind a delightful little garden which was presented to the people of the parish. A profusion of flowers grows beside the lake and waterfall, while opposite the church there is an arched well house crowned by a cross with a clover-shaped head. At the top of the village on the St Austell road we can see two of the several round thatched cottages which are a feature of the village. We drive from here to the little fishing harbour of Portloe, from which we have one of the best distant views of Dodman Point, driving up through the village from the cove.

We neglect the first turning on the right, taking the second for St Austell, next bearing right by a post box into a minor road. We are still proceeding towards St Austell, turning right at a T-junction, very soon right at a fork for Caerhays, Gorran and Mevagissey, right at a T-junction for Caerhays, and finally fork left. These somewhat complicated directions lead to one of the loveliest coves in Cornwall, Porthluney, a perfect place for bathing and picnicking with a spacious car park by the beach, surrounded by wooded slopes, dense to the west but green with graceful clumps of trees on the east. This is all part of the magnificent demesne of Caerhays Castle, a romantic-looking castellated mansion built early in the nineteenth century by John Nash and standing high among the trees behind an ornamental lake.

We shall probably be tempted to linger in this heavenly spot. When we leave we go on for Gorran and Mevagissey, coming first to Gorran Haven (the village of Gorran Churchtown lies just off the road to the left before we turn down to the Haven). Here we find another fishing village which has become a popular resort mainly on account of its broad sands. We can follow the road through the centre, passing the church on our right and bearing left at a fork to bring us back to the junction in the newer part of the village, where we turn right, and at the top of the hill right again for Mevagissey. Bear left at a vine-clad cottage and soon join a wide road from which we have a splendid coastal view before we drop down into Portmellon and drive round the inviting cove and up the opposite hill, at the top beginning the long steep descent into Mevagissey.

We wind through the maze of little streets to Mevagissey harbour, where we can drive right round the quayside to a car park, from which there is an extensive vista northwards along the coast towards Black Head. Return to the town and leave by the cliff road to the north, keeping right at all junctions to reach the next accessible beach along the coast at Pentewan, where we drive through the spacious village centre for Porthpean. The latter is signposted on the right after a good two miles, a tiny resort with a small beach and yacht club. After this we return to the major road and continue to St Austell, at A390 turning right, and right again at a large roundabout for Charlestown.

Charlestown is the port for St Austell, the centre of the china clay industry, and is memorable for its pleasant Georgian terrace above the high walls of the harbour with its china clay shutes. Return to the roundabout and drive into St Austell as far as the centre near the church, which has an elaborate tower with sculptured figures on each side and four clock faces. From the south side of the church in High Cross Street take the Plymouth road uphill past the Georgian Friends' Meeting House on the left and the contemporary-style library on the right (a striking contrast), and later cross the railway for Bethel and St Blazey. We soon cross a major road right-handed, in half a mile passing the Bethel Chapel dated 1838, and at the next hamlet turn right to join the Lostwithiel road (A390) into St Blazey.

At St Blazey's ancient church turn sharp right and shortly left over a level crossing at Par, famous for its sands, and forward for Tywardreath, turning left where the latter is again signposted. Drive through the village to St Andrew's church, which apart from the tower was rebuilt late in the nineteenth century, and then bear right towards Golant. We leave the Golant road, however, at the next crossroads and turn right on to the B3269 for Fowey, taking the left fork by a monolith for Fowey station. As we drive through the narrow streets of this traditionally important town at the mouth of the river Fowey, we can see numerous signs of its age-old prosperity in the splendid houses and public buildings ranging from medieval times to the eighteenth century, notably St Catherine's Castle, one of Henry VIII's coastal defences, the medieval church, and Place House. The ferry goes across the river from Fowey station to Bodinnick, and the finest vistas up and down river are seen during the crossing. We retrace our way to the junction by the monolith and then keep on B3269 to Lostwithiel, joining A390 for the last mile into the town.

Lostwithiel is a fascinating small town in a woodland setting by the Fowey river, which is here crossed by a fine medieval bridge. The church of St Bartholomew has an unusual lantern spire and a splendid east window, while the font is embellished by quaint figures and animals, including a knight on horseback blowing a horn and carrying a hawk, with a hound at his foot. There are some ancient houses and handsome Georgian ones in the town, which we leave by returning to A390. But before resuming our route we must make a detour to Restormel Castle, signposted just beyond the Talbot Hotel off A390. The castle ruins (open daily) date from the twelfth century, surrounded by a circular curtain wall, and are worth seeing not only because of their antiquarian interest but also for the beautiful surroundings, seen to good advantage on the mile drive up to the castle.

On returning to A390 turn right into it and take the second turning on the right, ascending to a hamlet and there by the pump turning right on the Bodmin road. Another mile brings us to the crossroads at the entrance to Lanhydrock, a seventeenth-century mansion with lovely gardens, the original North Wing of which is shown to visitors on Wednesday and Saturday afternoons from April to September.

We take the Truro road opposite the entrance, in less than half a mile turning right where Truro is again signposted. Our next junction is a six-way one where there is an inscribed granite shaft and at another point the wheel-head of Reperry Cross. We turn half right along an unsignposted lane which leads to Lanivet, famous for the Celtic crosses in its churchyard. The most impressive is a wheel-head cross over ten feet high and carved with the characteristic interlacings, while a more crude cross shows a man with a tail. In addition there is a stone inside the church inscribed with the Roman letters ANNICU FIL. We return to the six-way junction and there take the St Austell road by the wheel-head cross.

From this point we are going to see a district of Cornwall that may not appeal to all but is interesting to visit because there is nowhere else quite like it—the concentration of china clay works and their huge snowy-white spoil pyramids, a fantastic surrealist landscape. We follow the Luxulyan road for a time until we reach a turning for Roche and Bugle on the right, then continue for both places, crossing a major road by a chapel where St Austell is signposted and after crossing a stream milky-white with sediment and a railway, we turn right for Bugle and Roche. Now we are in the heart of the china clay works, with vast pyramids and milky pools, as we bear right on a major road, the B3374, and cross the main road, the A391, through the centre of Bugle for Carbis and Roche.

Roche is a remarkable place, its name derived from the huge rock mass crowned by a ruined chapel built for a hermit in the fifteenth century. Turn left beyond the rock and pass the church on our right as we drive out of the village. This is a handsome church with a tall tower but its chief feature of interest is the fine Norman font, embellished with heads on the four columns and intertwined snakes and foliage on the bowl. Our road climbs to the summit of Hensbarrow Downs, and we go forward for St Austell at the first junction and right at the crossroads on the descent where Whitemoor is signposted, continuing to Whitemoor, where we turn left, then right in a few yards for St Dennis, in less than a mile reaching the outskirts of the village. At St Dennis turn left then right and climb up to the little church over 600 ft up inside an Iron Age entrenchment. It looks over a curious landscape, a network of low stone walls dividing tiny fields.

We retrace our way through the village, keeping right at a fork near its end and later turning right for St Stephens. Thereafter the signposts take us without fail to this village on the main road. Turn right past the imposing church, which has a Norman font similar to that at Roche, and at the main road, A3058, turn right towards Newquay. After just over half a mile we must look for a left turn immediately after we have crossed a stream and follow this road for Grampound and Truro, bearing right for Grampound Road and left at a T-junction, soon crossing the railway at Grampound Road. We reach the main road, the A390, in a long mile from the station and turn right in it for Probus and Truro. Before we reach the former a turning to the right at a crossroads leads to the Georgian house of Trewithen. The house is open to visitors on Monday afternoons during the summer months, while the gardens are open on Tuesday and Thursday afternoons from March to June and in September.

Probus has suffered little from its position on the main road, and at one side of its open square surrounded by attractive houses is the church with its richly decorated tower in the 'Somerset' style soaring above all. From there we return to Truro and Falmouth.

Tour two: Helford river, Lizard peninsula

The second tour explores the Helford river and the Lizard peninsula, a distance of about 95 miles if the start is from Falmouth or Penryn, about 110 miles from Truro.

We drive along Falmouth's front, bear right at the Queen Mary Gardens and beyond the tennis courts turn left to obtain a high viewpoint to Pendennis Point and St Anthony Head across Carrick Roads and to Pennance Point ahead. On rejoining the major road turn left to Swanpool and Swanpool beach. From here we go inland temporarily until we turn left towards the sea at a T-junction where Maenporth and Mawnan are signposted, a road which brings us alongside Maenporth's sandy beach. Soon after passing through Meudon turn left for Mawnan church, a detour of just over half a mile worth making, not only for its ecclesiastical interest but also for the grand view from the church-yard across the mouth of the Helford river to Nare Point.

On our return to the junction bear left for Mawnan Smith, at its centre turning left for Helford Passage, and left again at a crossroads for Durgan. This road takes us through beautiful hanging woods down to the tiny settlement and beach on the shore of the Helford river, where we find the entrance to Glen-durgan Gardens, wonderfully landscaped along the valley and densely planted with many varieties of trees and shrubs. It is open to visitors on Mondays and Wednesdays from April to September, and occasionally also on Fridays. Once again we must retrace our way as far as the first junction, where we turn left for Helford Passage and left again to reach this village by the Helford river passenger ferry. We can drive a little way along a shelf road above the shore to a turning place, rewarded by extended views along the estuary, before returning through the village and turning left for Port Navas.

We round the heads of two wooded creeks before reaching

Port Navas, delightfully situated at the head of a third creek, and as we rise from water-level the views are most attractive. Constantine is our next objective, signposted at each junction, and we turn left into it towards the church, already seen before the turn. Not surprisingly, the granite church is dedicated to

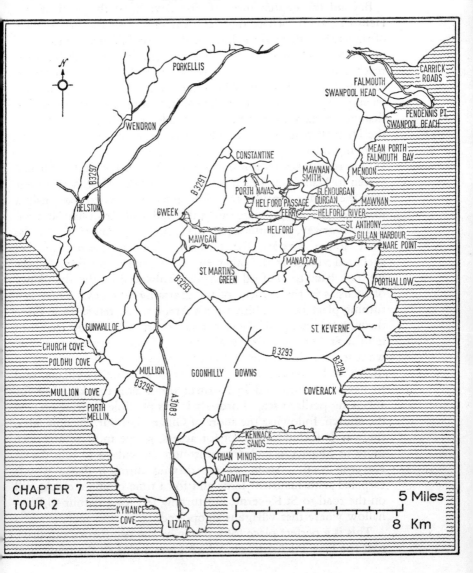

CHAPTER 7
TOUR 2

St Constantine and has a lofty tower and spacious interior, and, less obviously, to the left of the high altar, a good monumental brass showing a sixteenth-century family, which was evidently engraved on the reverse of part of an earlier one, shown in a framed rubbing.

Beyond the church turn left for Gweek, at the head of the Helford estuary, where there is a car park near the first branch of the creek. Beyond the head of the second branch we turn left on the St Keverne road, climbing through dense woods until we reach a junction by a war memorial at the top of the hill, where we turn left for Mawgan-in-Meneage, and after passing a tiny triangular green with a monolith in its centre and surrounded by thatched cottages, we come to the handsome church as we follow the Helford road, soon rounding two arms of a long creek and climbing inland again through woodlands.

Our road takes us through the smaller village of St Martin's Green to Manaccan, which is well signposted. Here we turn left into the village towards the high-set church, where curiously a massive fig tree is growing out of the wall near the simple Norman south doorway. Continue past the church to the next crossroads, there going forward for Helford. The appearance of this sheltered village at the other end of the passenger ferry (where we look back to Helford Passage) is enhanced by the abundance of fuchsias in the gardens of the charming cottages. There is a turning place by the Shipwright's Arms, so we return from there through the village to the crossroads short of Manaccan and turn left for St Anthony (also in Meneage). In little more than a mile we reach the tiny fishing harbour, where boats are drawn up on the shore beside the little church far away from its village, said to have been founded in Norman times as a thanksgiving for surviving perils at sea. Formerly it was possible to drive on past the church, following the shore of Gillan Harbour but now, alas, the way is forbidden except for access, so we must return once more to Manaccan and drive through the village to join the St Keverne road. Again we are driving through dense woods carpeted with luxuriant ferns and for a time beside a creek, still on the road to St Keverne, but turning left for a detour to Porthallow where that village is signposted.

This is a perfect place for a picnic by the sea, for we can drive past the Five Pilchards inn, which gives a clue to the traditional

fishing industry, and over a little stream trickling through the
pebbles to park right on the beach among the fishing boats and
lobster pots of the rock-girt cove. We return to the major road
for St Keverne, now only a short distance away, and soon enter
its spacious central square, surrounded by inns, pleasant houses,
and the large spired church. We leave the square by the Coverack
road (B3293) and later follow the B3294 all the way to Coverack,
a favourite resort with a fine sandy beach, though a rocky shore.

From Coverack we return to the first junction and turn left for
Helston, at the next major road turning left for the Lizard,
driving over Goonhilly Downs and turning left again for the
Lizard in sight of the prominent installations of the Post Office
Satellite Communication Earth Station. (A public viewing
enclosure is provided for the scientifically minded, reached by
going forward over the crossroads for a short distance.)

Several lanes lead from our road to the sea as we continue to
the Lizard, one to Kennack Sands, another to Cadgwith via Ruan
Minor, but at this stage we shall probably prefer to drive on to
the Lizard, following the signposts to the lighthouse and the
'most southerly point', where there is a car park from which we
can enjoy the magnificent cliff landscape and watch the waves
dashing endlessly against the dark rocks.

We must return to the main road for Helston, passing on the
left the track that leads towards the car park for Kynance Cove,
another grand rocky bay, and continuing for another two miles
as far as the left turn on to the B3296 for Mullion. When we
reach Mullion we drive on to its famous cove at Porth Mellin.
There is a car park in a large quarry before we arrive at the cove,
for the last few yards must be covered on foot. On regaining the
village drive past the church and take the road to Poldhu Cove, a
broad sandy expanse with ample car parking space, there following the road inland to rejoin the Helston road. The cliff road
leads to a viewpoint from which we can look down on Church
Cove and the little church of Gunwalloe among the sand dunes,
but unfortunately the road is not made up over the headland, and
the cove can only be reached by a turning farther along the
Helston road.

Turn left on B3293 into Helston, the town celebrated for the
Floral, or Furry, Dance traditionally observed on 8 May, when
gaily-dressed couples dance through the town, in and out of the

houses and shops. Helston has an imposing early Victorian town hall in the classical style and a handsome Georgian church, while the Gothic gateway and lodge at the foot of the High Street is a late Georgian memorial. Leave Helston by the Redruth road (B3297), going through Wendron, noting at the church the massive arched stone lych gate with a room above reached by outside steps. Beyond Wendron turn right by a stream for Porkellis, turning left at a T-junction near a tin mine chimney and right in the village by the Star inn, and thence continue for Penryn and Falmouth, keeping right at a fork.

For Truro we can either return on the main road, or branch off for Stithians, a pleasant alternative which brings us to the main road at Canron Downs, three miles short of Truro.

Tour three: Land's End

The third tour visits the Land's End peninsula and the many delightful coves and fishing villages along its coast. From Falmouth the distance covered is about 110 miles.

From Falmouth drive alongside the harbour to Penryn, turning left at the traffic lights to go through the ancient town and passing its picturesque town hall and many old houses of various periods. From Penryn take B3291 for Gweek and Helston, an excellent minor road which eventually bring us to a junction with B3293 at an aerodrome, where we turn right and shortly turn right again into the main road to Helston, the A3083.

In Helston's centre turn left towards Penzance and left by the memorial at the bottom of the High Street, and at the cattle market turn left again on B3304 for Porthleven. We drive right round Porthleven's capacious fishing harbour, neglecting the B road to Penzance and taking the lesser road, which brings us in two and a quarter miles to Ashton on the main road. We pass two turnings for Prah (or Praa) Sands and in just over another mile turn left opposite the Falmouth Packet inn for Prussia Cove, crossing Rosudgeon Common and following a winding lane down to a free car park which connects with coastal footpaths to several coves and beaches, an ideal place to spend a day or half a day.

Resuming our way on the main road towards Penzance, in little over two miles we arrive at Marazion, facing the romantic St Michael's Mount, accessible at low tide. The lovely home of

Lord St Levan, incorporating the surviving monastic buildings of the priory founded by Edward the Confessor, is open to visitors all the year on Wednesdays and Fridays, and in addition on Mondays from June to September. From Marazion we drive between the sea and a reedy lake and marsh on the right marked on the map as a submerged forest, soon coming to Penzance, and turning right to see its main street dominated by the handsome classical Lloyd's Bank on an island site with a statue of Humphrey Davy in front. We turn left towards the harbour, passing many Georgian houses, the church of St Mary the Virgin of the same period in the Gothic style, and the Customs House. A convenient car park is situated near the railway station and pier.

From the pier we drive along the promenade beside the ornamental gardens, keeping left and crossing a stream to go through Newlyn, where we pass the fish market and colourful harbour. We continue on a fine corniche road all the way to Mousehole, looking across to the inshore St Clement's Isle. Mousehole is a village of quaint corners and narrow twisting streets rising from its harbour, famous for crabs and lobsters, and, like Lamorna, beloved by artists and photographers. After

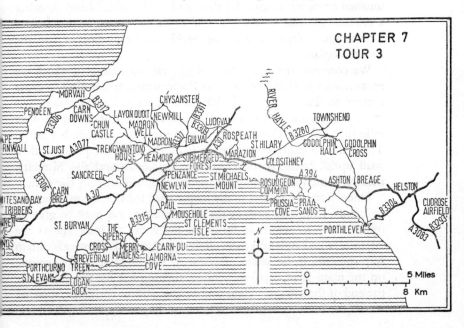

weaving our way down to the harbour take the road opposite the war memorial, rising steeply to Paul. Paul has two claims to fame, first, the two ancient crosses, one with a solid wheel-head just before the church and the head of another showing a crucifixion embedded in the church wall, the second, the grave of Dorothy Pentreath, who died in 1777 and is believed to have been the last person to speak the Cornish language. The memorial stone was erected by Prince Louis Bonaparte.

Immediately beyond the church turn left for Lamorna, turning left again on B3315, which runs through lovely woods. To reach the famous cove turn left once more down a densely wooded glen and past the Wink inn to the tiny rocky harbour, where there are car parks, and we look across to the castle-like headland of Carn-du.

About three-quarters of a mile after we have regained the major road, we look across the fields to our right for two huge standing stones, known as the Pipers, a little farther on the left an ancient cross, and just beyond that in a field, also on the left, the complete stone circle known as the Merry Maidens. This is not all, for in less than half a mile, opposite the St Buryan turning, we find an unusual cross with a circular shaft and a solid wheel-head showing a crucifixion, and finally a simple cross on the right just before Trevedran. Truly a feast of prehistoric monuments for the archaeologist.

We continue through a belt of natural woodland, in which we cross a stream, then turn left for Porthcurno, descending to cross a river to Treen, where a cliff walk of about half a mile starts from the inn just off the road to the Logan Stone. In another mile turn left for Porthcurno, where there is a telegraph station. There is a footpath to the beach from the large car park, while a road uphill leads to the church of St Levan and the Minnack theatre, which incorporates a natural amphitheatre in the cliff.

Once more we return to the major road for the last mile or two to Land's End, and here again there is a vast car park to give an opportunity to scramble down to the rocks to look across the Atlantic from England's most westerly point, and afterwards obtain refreshments if we wish. Return to the junction and continue on the main road (A30) to Sennen, turning left for the cove near the end of the village. Here too we can park near the sea, looking across the inviting sands of Whitesand Bay to Cape Cornwall and

Landscape near Boscastle.   (Chapter 8.)

Trebarwith Strand and Gull Rock.   (Chapter 8.)

Fistral Bay, Newquay.   (Chapter 8.)

Padstow Harbour.   (Chapter 8.)

watching the fascinating sea birds on the inshore rocks, The Tribbens. When we return to the main road we are high above the sea and we keep as near the coast as possible by forking left off the main road on to the B3306 where St Just is signposted. The peak of Carn Brea (657 ft) stands up boldly from the surrounding plateau, where prehistoric monuments are numerous.

We continue to St Just-in-Penwith through a countryside divided into small fields bounded by the typical Cornish stone walls where small Guernsey herds graze. St Just is an exceptionally spacious village with two squares, the first near the church where the old market house, now the Wellington Hotel, stands on the corner, and the second with a clock tower war memorial and a handsome classical Wesleyan chapel at the far end. From the clock tower a detour may be made to Cape Cornwall.

We drive through on the Zennor road, passing the ruined buildings of many disused tin and copper mines, and later we see the gear of a working mine in Pendeen. Pendeen's church is modelled on Iona Cathedral and was designed in the middle of last century by the then vicar, and built of granite quarried by the villagers. The next village on our route is Morvah, where we leave the major road after passing the church, forking right for Madron and driving over Carn downs, with Chun Castle, an Iron Age hilltop fort, seen to our right on the skyline. This fort is the centre of another group of prehistoric settlements and monuments, and in under two miles from Morvah we pass on our left Lanyon Quoit, one of the finest of the Neolithic burial chambers, an enormous capstone crowning three standing stones.

A rhododendron-lined road leads us to a signposted junction where to the left a footpath starts for the old holy well (now called a wishing well) inside the ruins of a chapel. We go forward into Madron, where the fine medieval church is the mother church of Penzance (St Madernus), and drive through the pleasant village to the crossroads beyond, there turning left at Heamoor for Gulval. (The road on the right leads in half a mile to the beautiful Trengwainton Gardens, open March to September on Wednesdays, Fridays and Saturdays, and beyond the gardens to the village of Sancreed, which has an exceptionally interesting church. From the church we can proceed to the point in half a mile where the Iron Age village of Carn Euny is signposted. It is well worth following the signposts and taking the short walk to see this wonderful survival, with its 60-ft secret passage.)   Continuing our route from Heamoor, in a mile we turn left for Newmill and beyond this (in about two miles) right at the Ancient Monument sign for Chysauster, the footpath to which we soon reach, and this remarkable Iron Age village is well worth the short walk.   There are a number of stone houses, each with several rooms, dating from the first century B.C. to the third century A.D.

The road leads on past Chysauster to Gulval, a winding lane through a well-timbered landscape, and we soon enter Gulval, where we keep the church on our right, going on for Ludgvan, neglecting a left turn where our road narrows.   On the village outskirts bear left down to a major road, there turning right to cross a stream into the village, where we cross A30 for Rospeath. We cross a pleasant fertile valley, turning right towards Marazion, which brings us to the main road, where we turn left towards Helston for half a mile, then left on B3280 for Goldsithney and St Hilary, driving through the long village street of the former and skirting the latter as we go down to cross the river Hayle. At a crossroads in Townshend turn right for Breage and Helston, soon recrossing the river and driving through the well-timbered park of Godolphin Hall.   The entrance is on the right of the road before we leave the woods, and we may care to note that the Tudor house is open to visitors during the summer months on Thursday afternoons, and in August and September on Tuesday afternoons as well.

At Godolphin Cross we make for Helston via Breage and thence return to Falmouth or Truro.

CHAPTER EIGHT

NORTH CORNWALL

THE NORTH COAST of Cornwall is just as popular as the south, conjuring up pictures of Atlantic breakers rolling in to dash against rocky headlands or spend themselves on the wide sandy beaches. Almost every fishing village has become a holiday resort, as well as the larger towns which have grown up mainly to cater for holiday-makers. The following tours, therefore, can be joined from any point along the coast, as well as from inland towns such as Launceston and Bodmin.

The first two tours are routed from Newquay, which is an excellent centre and has almost limitless accommodation. Even this gay resort sprang from a former fishing village and the ancient Huer's House on the headland recalls the time when the huer's job was to watch for the arrival of the pilchard shoals. Only three miles away the Elizabethan house of Trerice is seen by many Newquay visitors, for it is open on Wednesdays, Thursdays and Sundays from April to September. The mellow stone house has distinctive shaped gables and the hall, which extends through two storeys, has an enormous window divided into twenty-four lights. Trerice is reached by a right turn at Kestle Mill off A3058, and we can return via Trewerry Mill (1630), where the wheel is still in place, and Newlyn East.

Tour one: Holywell, St Ives, St Erth

Our first tour follows the coast in a south-westerly direction as far as St Ives, and can just as easily start from that famous resort. It covers approximately 110 miles. We leave Newquay by the Redruth road (A3075), and soon after passing Trenance ornamental lake and gardens turn right for Pentire Point West and Crantock. From there the signposts take us over the two and a half miles to West Pentire, a charming little group of inns and cottages round a tiny green, from which there are fine views over Crantock sands and up the Gannel estuary. On the return drive into Crantock village (by-passed on our way to West Pentire), where from the centre a lane leads to the beach and a large car park by the sand dunes marked as the Rushy Glen National Trust property. In the village itself the bow-windowed post office and the two inns, the thatched and colour-washed Old Albion next to the church lych gate and the newer Seagull opposite, make picturesque corners. The church has a simple rough-cast exterior but has been tastefully restored inside.

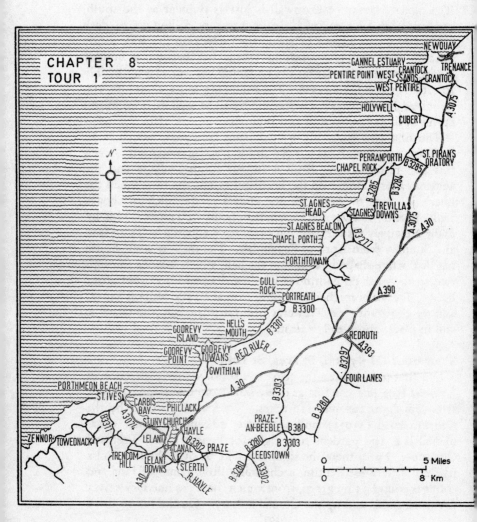

We resume our route at the crossroads, there taking Trevowah
Road for Cubert, marked ahead by a spire on the hilltop. When
we arrive at the village we leave the church to our left, passing
another bow-windowed post office, and go on to Holywell,
which takes its name from a well on the beach, and where there
are good sands. The footpath leads from a point just beyond the
attractive thatched Treguth inn and its adjacent buildings.

On leaving Holywell make for Perranporth, turning right less
than half a mile beyond Cubert to the Smugglers' Den (the
turning is otherwise unsignposted). This is a quiet and adventurous little lane which takes us all the way to Perranporth
without touching the main road, and although it is a winding
single track way at first, it later joins a wider road, in which we
turn right. The road now passes behind an extensive area of
dunes containing the ancient ruin of St Piran's oratory, marked
by a stone cross, considered by some authorities to be the oldest
chapel in England. It can only be reached on foot by a path over
the sands.

We join a major road, the B3285, into Perranporth, noted for
its magnificent sands and Atlantic breakers ideal for surf-riding.
The inshore Chapel Rock and the rock arch to the south-west add
interest to the scene. From the clock tower keep right alongside
the little stream and garden on the St Agnes road, soon climbing
over Trevellas Downs before reaching the centre of St Agnes.
A pretty road to the right leads down to the beach and a small
car park by the lifeboat. The many ruined buildings and
chimneys of the former tin workings surrounding St Agnes give
a clue to its traditional industry and its former prosperity, while
the harbour by the lifeboat was used for shipping the tin.

In the town follow the one-way system, making for the spired
church via British Road and turning right at the T-junction at the
top. Opposite the church turn left for Beacon, bearing left at a
fork and driving through old tin workings, thence following
Beacon Drive. From the car park near the summit of the
Beacon, which rises to over 600 ft, there is a magnificent view
forward along the coast to St Ives, scarcely less impressive than
that from the actual summit, reached by a footpath. We pass a
signpost to Wheal Coates, and may have noticed other Wheal
signs followed by a woman's name, such as Wheal Kitty. The
word 'wheal' means a mine and, like ships, the mines were given

women's names. The signposted ways, therefore, lead to old mine buildings.

Proceed round the Beacon to the Porthtowan turning on the right, disregarding the Chapel Porth turn, and keep right again at the Victory inn to follow Coast Road, looking ahead to Godrevy island and lighthouse. We soon descend steeply to Porthtowan's sandy cove, reached along Beach Road at the foot of the hill. Ruined tin mine buildings stand by the shore, adding a picturesque note rather than detracting from the scene. On regaining the major road turn right uphill for Portreath, later joining B3300 to drive along the wooded river valley that ends at Portreath's popular beach, which boasts a pier, and looks out to a large Gull Rock.

From Portreath's car park turn right up a sharp incline, keeping to the coast road (B3301) at a fork. The cliffs to the right of this grand road are in the care of the National Trust, and there are many parking places for those who wish to walk along the cliff paths to enjoy the superb views to St Agnes Head and Godrevy island in a more leisurely fashion. Soon after passing a signpost to Hell's Mouth the road descends to Godrevy Towans (a word meaning dunes) and crosses the Red river, which is literally that colour. Near this river is the little oratory of St Gothian buried in the sands, similar to St Piran's at Perranporth, and believed to be as old. We drive into its former parish of Gwithian, there turning right for Hayle, joining the main Camborne road into the town, a thriving and expanding one proud of its fine harbour and extensive sands. Its mother church is at nearby Phillack, signposted before the road passes the wide canal.

We drive alongside the canal and, after turning right under a viaduct twice for St Ives, beside the wide estuary of the Hayle river and rounding its head before turning right at Old Quay House into the Borough of St Ives. We first pass through Lelant, originally the mother parish of St Ives, where we leave the main road, going forward to the church of St Uny, which retains some Norman work as evidence of its early foundation. The road bends round to rejoin the main road into Carbis Bay and St Ives. The former is off the road to the right, a sandy cove sheltered by a high wooded cliff with parking space by the beach.

St Ives is often described as an artist's paradise, supported by the fact that according to scientific measurement it has the greatest amount of ultra-violet light in the country, and the numerous quaint corners in the little narrow streets provide an endless number of subjects for the artist. Although the church was not built as a parish church it is a splendid fifteenth-century structure with a high tower, and in the churchyard there is a fine lantern cross on a tall shaft. It stands beside the harbour near the lifeboat and old Customs House.

Other interesting features in St Ives are the pier built by Smeaton, the Georgian Treganna Castle, now an hotel, and St Nicholas Chapel on a hill above the sea. A curiosity on the hillside above Carbis Bay is the Knill monument, a pointed structure resembling an elongated steeple built late in the eighteenth century by John Knill, a former mayor of the town. It is worth parking and walking round the little streets on foot to savour the atmosphere of the town. Care has been taken when rebuilding or extending old buildings that the new blends with the old in perfect harmony and the use of slate hanging gives a homogeneous appearance to many streets.

When we leave St Ives, no doubt with regret, take the Zennor road past Porthmeon beach and from there follow the signposts to Zennor (Land's End is also signposted) over high downs rising to summits on our left. At Zennor turn right at the sign of the Tinner's Arms to the church and a 'wayside folk museum', a collection of bygones and items of local interest. The legendary Mermaid of Zennor is shown on an old bench end in the church as well as on the inn sign. We continue past the cottage garden museum to rejoin the main road, and in about a mile and a half turn left for Gulval over open moorland with a remarkable view to the Lizard on days of clear visibility. After a mile over the breezy moorland turn left towards Zennor and on reaching the main road again turn right, passing Zennor to the left and after two miles turn right for Towednack. Beyond the little village turn left for Lelant Downs, shortly crossing a major road left-handed as we go on for Hayle.

As we proceed towards Hayle we see on the left of our road the huge Bowl Rock, according to folklore used by giants playing a game on the wooded Trencrom Hill rising high to our right. On joining a main road near Hayle turn right, keep right for Penzance in a few yards, then right once more on A30, again signposted Penzance. We soon leave the main road, however, in just over a quarter of a mile turning left beside the railway station for St Erth. This is a pretty and very ancient village with some interesting features, including the mellow medieval stone bridge over the river Hayle, and several early crosses.

We join a wider road, the B3302, at Praze, thence continuing to the crossroads at Leedstown, where we turn left on to the B3280 for Praze an Beeble (a convenient point for Camborne motorists to join the tour), going forward at the tree-shaded green for Four Lanes. Now continue to Redruth, joining B3297 and turning left at the junction with A393 into the town, which has a modern look though there are some handsome late eighteenth-century and early Victorian buildings. At the centre take the Bodmin road, forking left for Newquay after several miles and thereafter following the signposted way to Newquay.

Tour two: Padstow, Bodmin

The second tour, of about eighty miles, goes northwards along the coast to Padstow and returns via Bodmin, the county town. We leave Newquay by the main road from the front eastwards, shortly turning left on the B3276 for St Columb Porth, where we drive alongside the sands, looking forward to Trevelgue Head and back to Towan Head. After crossing the narrow peninsula behind Trevelgue Head our road keeps close to the coast and we turn left for Watergate and Bedruthan Steps to bring us down to shore level to look along the wide sandy expanse of Watergate beach. Still keeping to the coast go forward for Trevarrian and Mawgan Porth.

Mawgan Porth lies at the foot of the beautiful Vale of Lanherne, where the river Mellanhayle flows down to the sea through splendid woods. To see part of this valley turn right after crossing the river at Mawgan Porth and drive up the valley, soon rounding a steep hairpin bend. After about a mile and a half take the second turning on the right for Mawgan (-in-Pydar) and descend steeply through woods to the riverside village in its lovely wooded setting. The church is a particularly interesting one, its high tower soaring among the trees capped by a pinnacled stair turret. The Norman bowl font on five pillars is its oldest feature, and it has a fine screen and some good brasses and slate memorial slabs. In the churchyard there are several crosses, especially a medieval lantern cross with figures carved on each side.

On the other side of the church wall we find the Roman
Catholic Carmelite convent at Lanherne, the home of the Arundell
family, given by the then Lord Arundell to refugee nuns from the
French Revolution, and outside its little chapel an inscribed
Celtic cross with a crucifixion on its wheel-head.

We recross the bridge to leave the village and continue forward
uphill to the main road, where the way is to the left to regain the
coast road at Mawgan Porth, and there right for Trenance and
Bedruthan Steps.   At the top of the steep hill turn left for
Trenance, from that point our road continuing at a high level
above the cliffs.   The extensive vista on our right is bounded by
Bodmin Moor, and forward along the coast by the jutting
headland of Trevose.

A mile beyond Trenance a track leads to the fantastic caves and

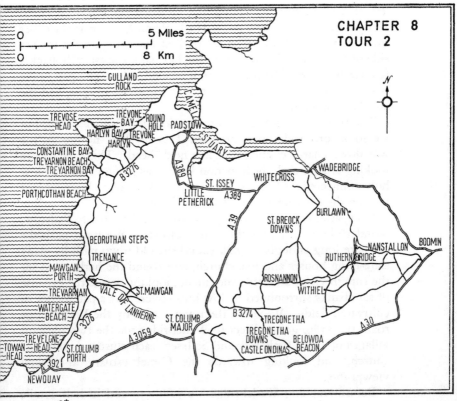

stack rocks of Bedruthan, which unfortunately can only be reached on foot over the cliffs, but it is well worth making the effort to see this unique formation, a truly awesome spectacle when the sea is rough and the foaming waves lash the dark rocks. From here our way is signposted Padstow at two junctions and then the road descends to Porthcothan and crosses a stream near the sands. A short way up the ascending slope we turn left for Treyarnon, to which we continue. The tamarisk hedges typical of North Cornwall are especially luxuriant on this part of the coast. Treyarnon's beach is another extensive sandy one, reached by a signposted road. We return to the junction and turn left for Constantine Bay, at the highest point of our road looking forward to Trevose Head. Constantine's beach and dunes are the last that can be reached before we turn inland behind Trevose Head for Padstow, but we soon leave the Padstow road again after turning left at a T-junction by taking the road on the left signposted Harlyn Bay, now looking out to the Gulland Rock from the other side of Trevose Head. The car park at Harlyn is on the farther side of the stream that runs into the bay, so we must walk back a few yards to see an Iron Age burial ground, where an open grave is shown, a site of immense interest to the archaeologist, and the attached museum.

The road continues from here to rejoin the Padstow road, but we soon turn aside once more for Trevone Bay, noting on the way down a large circular hole in a field ahead. This time we are looking at a natural phenomenon known as Round Hole, a blow hole connected with the sea by a cave. We get a closer look at it from the car park overlooking the beach.

Now, after regaining the major road, we drive on into Padstow, wonderfully situated on the Camel estuary. We must park the car here long enough to walk round the old town with its many slate-hung houses and fine church, and round the harbour to see the superb views seawards and inland, looking across the expanse of sandbanks surrounded by low hills covered by a patchwork of cultivated fields. We leave the town centre by the Wadebridge road, the A389, going direct to Wadebridge via the two pleasant villages of Little Petherick and St Issey, each clustered round its church, and looking towards the Camel estuary at several viewpoints.

Before reaching Wadebridge we join A39 and in half a mile

drive through White Cross, which actually has on the wayside to the right a wheel-head on a short shaft with the low relief cross painted white. Soon after passing a former tollhouse with Gothic-style windows we enter the town, a typical one with some gracious Georgian houses and a Regency hotel, the Molesworth Arms, embellished with a handsome painted coat of arms over its pillared porch. But the glory of Wadebridge is the splendid fifteenth-century bridge of seventeen arches across the Camel, still doing as good service as it did when it was first built by the then vicar of Egloshayle, Thomas Lovibond. Our route does not go as far as the bridge, for we turn right in the High Street before reaching the level crossing and go straight on in this minor road, at a crossroads still going forward for Withiel. This brings us on to an open moorland road over St Breock Downs, and at a high point turn left towards a strange skyline of pyramids denoting the china clay district north of St Austell. After this junction we descend beside a valley on the left towards a more fertile landscape broken up by woodland.

We turn aside from the Withiel road, continuing downhill for Ruthern and Bodmin, crossing the medieval two-arched Ruthern-bridge by a pretty corner of the riverside hamlet, and follow the signposts into Bodmin, turning right at a fork where Truro is signposted to join A30 into Bodmin. Bodmin is the county town of Cornwall and has a long history going back to the sixth century when St Petrock is believed to have founded a monastery here, and on his death a shrine was erected over his bones. Of this and the later Benedictine priory virtually nothing survives, but the later fifteenth-century church of St Petrock is the largest and one of the loveliest in Cornwall, standing in a commanding position near the gardens and lake (where there is a good car park). Noteworthy among the many interesting features inside the church are the richly ornamented tomb of Prior Vyvyan, his effigy in full bishop's regalia, and the Norman font, outstanding in a county noted for its splendid fonts. Between the winged heads on the four corner columns the enormous bowl is ornamented with rich interwoven foliage and heads of beasts in high relief, artistically perfect in design and execution.

Most of Bodmin's public buildings, including the classical Assize Court, are nineteenth century, though there are earlier houses, especially in Fore Street. We leave the centre on A30 (the way we came in) but soon leave it after passing a clock tower on the right and the Abbey Church of St Mary and St Petrock on the left, taking a road on the right signposted Nanstallon, but in less than a quarter of a mile turn left into a rather obscure unsignposted lane. Follow this quiet little road for several miles through farmland, mainly pasture fields and woods, and later it is signposted Withiel at several points. After well over three miles we must watch for the signposted fork to the right by a wall letter box and we shortly descend into the hillside village dominated by the church tower, given added height by elaborate pinnacles, noting the fine window tracery as we drive past the church.

From Withiel bear left on the Wadebridge road, continuing downhill into a partly wooded valley with many mature trees and after crossing a stream turn right on the ensuing ascent, then immediately left for Burlawn to climb up to St Breock Downs. At the top turn left on the St Columb road, shortly going forward for the same destination, and again looking across to the china clay pyramids.

Two standing stones are etched against the sky to the right, the second on the highest point of the downs. It is worth taking the road to the 16-ft monolith with the double purpose of enjoying the grand view from the top as well as seeing the stone (the left fork is the better way to it). After resuming we pass an extensive plantation of deciduous trees on our left and shortly afterwards descend into the tiny hamlet of Rosnannon, at a junction just beyond it going forward and later right for St Columb. In a third of a mile, however, turn off towards Roche, driving through Tregonetha and over Tregonetha Downs, from which the Iron Age hilltop fort of Castle an Dinas can be seen to the right. Near the foot of Belowda Beacon (744 ft) turn right for Belowda and St Columb and after a mile join a wider road. Here we are over 500 ft up and at our closest point to Castle an Dinas, but from the road can get no real impression of its immense size and three circular ramparts.

The way is now straight ahead, neglecting all side turnings, until we come to the outskirts of St Columb Major, turning right twice to reach the centre. Here we shall find some interesting houses, such as Glebe House, dated 1638, and several elegant Georgian houses. The fourteenth-century Gothic moated Rectory beyond the imposing church is now a guest house, and there are an attractive row of houses and an old mill by the river at the foot of the town. From here we follow the signposts to Newquay.

The next two tours are routed from Bude, one of the larger resorts to the north. Its parish church is at neighbouring Stratton (probably named from the Roman 'street'), a town of many fine houses and thatched cottages, and a manor-house which has become the Tree inn.

Tour three: Tintagel, Camel estuary

The first tour from Bude or Stratton covers just over 100 miles, following the coast southwards beyond romantic Tintagel as far as the Camel estuary. From the beach at Bude cross the bridge and turn left on the farther side, climbing to a high view-point where we look over Widemouth Bay before descending to shore level beside the wonderful stretch of sands. From here we keep to the coast road for Millook and St Genny's, a switchback cliff road which needs bottom gear for much of the way, but gives superb vistas along the coast. There is a parking space at the top of the first hill where we can pause and enjoy the view north-wards over Widemouth Sand towards Hartland Point and Lundy Island. A narrow 1 in 3 hill descends from here to Millook and ascends equally steeply after crossing the combe. (It is possible to avoid this stiff road by turning inland from Widemouth to Crackington Haven but, of course, the coastal views are missed.)

Our coast road brings us eventually to a crossroads at Tremayna Methodist church, where we turn right, shortly afterwards taking a right fork for St Genny's beside a whitewashed cottage with a dovecot incorporated in the end wall. The little church of St Genny's forms a delightful group beside farm buildings high above the sea and is notable for the surviving Norman work, including part of the tower. We return to the fork by the cottage, taking the Crackington Haven road, and drive down to the haven, which is not only a resort but a place of interest to geologists who come to study its fantastic rock formations, especially the great slabs of rock on the shore which have collapsed like playing cards. To the west the haven is bounded by the characteristic triangular mass of Cambeak.

We climb up from Crackington Haven by the Trevigue road, a steep gated road which keeps close to the coast before turning inland to bring us to the Boscastle road at a high crossroads,

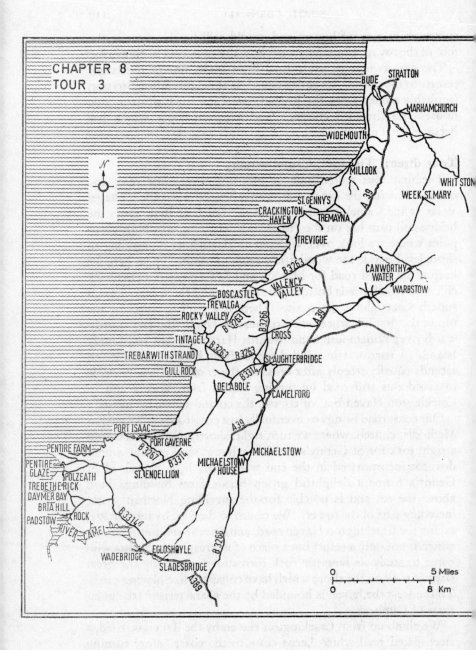

CHAPTER 8
TOUR 3

N

STRATTON
BUDE
MARHAMCHURCH
WIDEMOUTH
MILLOOK
WHIT STON
WEEK ST. MARY
ST. GENNY'S
CRACKINGTON HAVEN
TREMAYNA
TREVIGUE
CANWORTHY WATER
WARBSTOW
B 3263
VALENCY VALLEY
BOSCASTLE
TREVALGA
ROCKY VALLEY
B 3263
B 3266
CROSS
A 39
TINTAGEL
B 3263
B 3263
TREBARWITH STRAND
SLAUGHTERBRIDGE
GULL ROCK
B 3314
DELABOLE
CAMELFORD
A 39
PORT ISAAC
PORT GAVERNE
B 3267
B 3314
MICHAELSTOW
PENTIRE FARM
MICHAELSTOW HOUSE
PENTIRE GLAZE
POLZEATH
ST. ENDELLION
TREBETHERICK
DAYMER BAY
BRIA HILL
PADSTOW
B 3314
ROCK
RIVER CAMEL
B 3266
EGLOSHAYLE
WADEBRIDGE
SLADESBRIDGE
A 389

0   5 Miles
0   8 Km

where we turn right on the B3263 and follow the road into Boscastle. This is such a favourite village and harbour that it is worth parking the car and exploring on foot. There is, too, a footpath up the beautiful wooded Valency valley, following the course of the river which runs down to the harbour. The main street of the village leads from the Wellington hotel at the bridge to the Napoleon inn near the top, a street of many pretty white-washed cottages, and we can also walk down to the harbour, surely a navigator's nightmare, reached from the sea through a twisting rock-girt channel.

From the centre we take the Tintagel road, which rises above the harbour and doubles back by a hairpin bend to run parallel with the village, seen on the left through woodland. The parish church of St Symphorian is in a solitary position high on the cliff at Forrabury, which we can see by turning right off the major road up a steep hill and rejoining the main road half a mile before Trevalga, where the medieval church of St Petrock also stands high on the cliff. A mile beyond this we cross the wooded Rocky Valley, where it is possible to walk up the valley to a fine water-fall, and down to the sea beside the cascading stream (there is a parking space just beyond the Rocky Valley hotel).

Our next objective is one of the most celebrated in Cornwall, the romantic village of Tintagel which has grown up by the medieval castle. Although it is established that the castle was built in the twelfth century by Reginald, Earl of Cornwall, legend obstinately connects the castle with King Arthur. There are, however, on the island the slight remains of a Celtic monastery possibly founded in the fifth century, evidence of early occupation of the site, so there is nothing to disprove the fact that the headland may have been held at one time by Arthur. The castle is open daily to visitors on payment of a small fee.

On the way into the village we pass the old post office, a small fourteenth-century manor-house with a hall, now in the care of the National Trust and open on weekdays from March to October and on Sunday afternoons from May to September. We continue past King Arthur's Hall to reach the nearest car park to the castle beside the little Coin Museum.

After seeing the castle we retrace our way for a few yards and turn right just beyond the Avalon hotel and drive to the church half a mile away. This church of St Materiana is also believed to have links with early times, for the saint was in the locality in the sixth century and was buried at Minster a few miles away. The Norman church, believed to stand on the site of a sixth-century oratory, has survived in plan, though the tower was built in the fourteenth century, and there are three fine Norman windows and a primitive Norman font with faces at the corners. In the south transept an upright stone with a Latin inscription referring to the Roman Emperor Licinius is yet one more proof of occupation in the vicinity dating back to the fourth century.

The easiest way to resume our route is to return to Tintagel and turn right for Camelford opposite King Arthur's Hall, though there is a rough but passable track from the church which joins the major road half a mile beyond Tintagel. At all events we continue towards Camelford and soon plunge into a deep combe, turning right into it for Trebarwith Strand, a delightful sandy beach with rock pools and a massive Gull Rock standing offshore. Retracing our way to the major road, we turn right, and later right again for Delabole, then once more turn right again on to the B3314 where Port Isaac and Polzeath are signposted. Drive right through Delabole, famous for its slate quarries, noticing on the right the Bettle and Chisel inn, its sign showing a slate worker. Another three miles over the high plateau brings us to a crossroads where we turn right for Port Gaverne, which we come to before the road climbs up to the outskirts of Port Isaac, and half encircle its rocky cove.

A car park above Port Isaac gives a grand view along the coast to the Island of Tintagel, and it is good policy to leave the car there before going down into the narrow streets of picturesque cottages in Port Isaac, a village whose popularity as a holiday resort has overshadowed its former prominence as a fishing port. We leave Port Isaac by the major road (B3267) and turn right at the T-junction with B3314. We continue along this through St Endellion, passing its handsome church, where there is some fine stone carving to be seen, in particular a table tomb in slate-coloured stone with eight deep niches under beautiful arches round its sides.

A mile and a quarter beyond the church fork right for Pentire Glaze, a growing resort on Hayle Bay, beyond which lies the lovely Pentire headland. We cannot drive all the way, but can get as far as Pentire Farm (via a turning on the right beside farm buildings before we enter Pentire Glaze), where there is parking in the farmyard for a small charge, and walk along a grassy path to the headland.

We retrace our way as far as a turning on the right for Polzeath, where the sands are extensive and parking on the beach is allowed. We can continue over the hill on the farther side of the bay, driving through Trebetherick and down to Daymer Bay, where the sands cover the site of a submerged forest. Here again there is ample parking space for those who wish to linger and enjoy the vista across the Camel estuary over the level stretch of sand, bounded on the left by the dome-like Brea Hill. Returning to Trebetherick, turn right three times in succession for Rock before we drive down to this unspoilt corner facing Padstow across the Camel, a deservedly popular little resort. We return from here to the first junction, thence following the signposts to Wadebridge.

If we have previously visited Wadebridge there is no need to go into the town, but go straight on with the old bridge over the Camel on our right, following the Bodmin road (A389) through Egloshayle, where its commanding church looks over the river, and up a pretty wooded valley after Sladesbridge. About two and a half miles beyond Sladesbridge turn left on B3266, a pleasant road at first through woods then over pastoral landscapes. We continue on this road towards Camelford for over five miles, and then a mile after turning sharp right where a road goes forward to Michaelstow House, we watch for a crossroad sign which gives us our cue for a detour to Michaelstow along an obscure left turning by a building. The mellow old church stands high on the right at the top of a flight of steps surrounded by a small group of village houses and beyond it we turn right at a T-junction to regain the major road for Camelford, joining A39 into the centre.

Camelford is a compact small town chiefly centred on one main street, near the end of which the early nineteenth-century town hall surmounted by a clock tower stands on an island site. We continue beyond the town to the first crossroads, where we turn left, then right at a telephone box to cross the Camel by Slaughter Bridge, where, according to legend, King Arthur fought his last battle. This road brings us back to B3266 and we now proceed along it for one and a half miles to a crossroads where Bude is signposted to the right. Follow this downland road, passing the sculptured shaft of an old cross on the right in half a mile, until we rejoin A39 by a group of tumuli (prehistoric burial mounds) on both sides of the road. Leave the main road after a mile for a turning on the right signposted Launceston just short of a disused railway station and in about three-quarters of a mile turn left for Warbstow and Canworthy Water.

We bear right at the next junction, following the line of the disused railway, then left at a triangular junction, go over two crossroads (the second signposted Holsworthy), and turn right at a fork beside Warbstow Bury, a huge circular prehistoric fort. At the bottom of the hill a right turn at the war memorial leads to Warbstow village, but the way to Canworthy Water is straight on and after crossing the river Ottery there we fork left for Week St Mary, which is signposted to the right in just over a mile. The village has a surprisingly spacious centre and a cattle market nearby, and as we drive through it we pass the church on the left and an attractive triangular green, then take the right-hand road signposted Whitstone, once more driving through a fertile landscape of pasture fields and woods. After crossing a stream in a combe turn left for Marhamchurch, turning left again beyond a Victorian chapel, and right in little over a hundred yards.

Marhamchurch is another village grouped round a large open square, with the church at one end and near it some pretty thatched and colour-washed cottages. We leave it by the turning almost opposite the church, signposted Bude, turning right on reaching A39 and going forward in it briefly to the turning on the left for Bude (A3073).

Tour four: Morwenstowe, Kilkhampton

The second tour from Bude is a shorter one of little over sixty miles and visits the famous church of Morwenstowe near the Devon border and its equally fine near neighbour, Kilkhampton church, and follows the upper reaches of the Tamar for part of the return journey. We leave Bude by taking the road from the river towards Poughill, going forward at the top for Crooklets and down to Maer Lake cove, continuing from here through Flexbury to Poughill. (Motorists from Stratton can join the tour at this point.) In sight of Poughill church (dedicated to St Olaf, a Danish saint, strangely foreign among so many Celtic saints), we

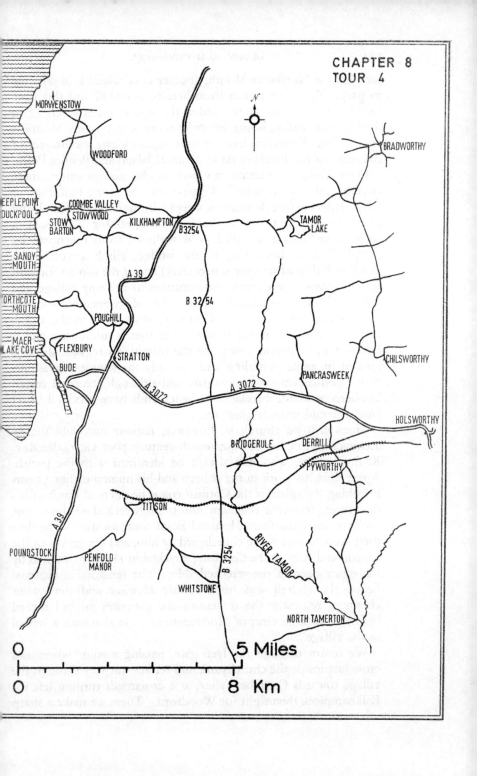

CHAPTER 8
TOUR 4

MORWENSTOW

WOODFORD

BRADWORTHY

EEPLEPOINT
UCKPOOL

COOMBE VALLEY
STOWWOOD

STOW
BARTON

KILKHAMPTON

B3254

TAMOR
LAKE

SANDY
MOUTH

A 39

B 32/54

ORTHCOTE
MOUTH

POUGHILL

MAER
LAKE COVE

FLEXBURY

BUDE

STRATTON

CHILSWORTHY

A 3072

A 3072

PANCRASWEEK

HOLSWORTHY

BRIDGERULE

DERRILL

PYWORTHY

A 39

TITSON

RIVER TAMOR

POUNDSTOCK

PENFOLD
MANOR

B 3254

WHITSTONE

NORTH TAMERTON

0   5 Miles

0   8 Km

turn left for Northcott Mouth, another cove where it is possible to park. We must return from here to Poughill and this time turn left to pass the church and at the next crossroads left again for Coombe Valley, going left twice more where Sandy Mouth is signposted. From this lane we have superb views southwards of the series of headlands as far as Tintagel Island and Pentire Point.

Once again we retrace our way to the first junction, there turning left for Coombe. We pass the old stone buildings of Stow Barton before descending steeply through Stowe Wood, and after crossing a stream at the foot turn left for Duckpool, a rocky cove with a sea-filled pool sheltered from the north by Steeple Point. Returning to the bridge, climb a very steep winding hill (bottom gear is necessary) and at the top go forward for Morwenstowe church and continue to the tiny village and famous church. The lovely church of St Morwenna has some of the best Norman carving in Cornwall, at its finest in the arches and capitals of the north arcade. The font is interesting and is believed to be Saxon work, for the primitive irregular shape is girdled by cable moulding and has only the simplest incisions. The wood carving is noteworthy and although the rood screen has been restored, the elaborate bench ends have survived intact from the mid-sixteenth century.

Morwenstowe church is, however, famous not only for its architecture but for the nineteenth-century poet-vicar, the Rev. R. S. Hawker, who will always be identified with the parish. Apart from his work in the church and his numerous fine poems breathing the spirit of the Cornish coast, he devoted much of his time trying to rescue the many sailors shipwrecked on the savage rocks of the coast from Hartland Point southwards. More than forty were buried in the churchyard by him, and the graves of the captain and crew of the *Caledonia*, wrecked in 1843, are marked by the figure-head of the wrecked ship. The remarkable vicarage below the church was built by Mr Hawker and the quaint chimneys represent the towers of the churches he had served before he became vicar of Morwenstowe. He also built a school in the village.

We return through the lych gate, passing a short wheelhead cross just inside the churchyard, and retrace our way through the village towards Coombe Valley, at a crossroads turning left for Kilkhampton, then right for Woodford. There we make a sharp

Launceston Castle.
(Chapter 8.)

The old Post Office,
Tintagel.   (Chapter 8.)

King Doniert's Stone,
nr St Cleer. (Chapter 8.)

Bodmin moor from the
Bodmin-Launceston road.
(Chapter 8.)

bend to the left and shortly cross a stream flowing between wooded banks, then climb steeply uphill, and after descending into another valley climb steadily to high-set Kilkhampton, turning right to the church. This is another splendid church, dedicated to St James, and entered by a magnificent Norman doorway. The interior is lofty and spacious and there is exceptionally good wood carving on the numerous bench ends.

Just beyond the church and the London inn turn left on B3254, and in half a mile leave this road by going straight forward on the minor road signposted Bradworthy, and in just over one and a half miles turn left where Bradworthy is again signposted. By this road into Bradworthy we cross the end of the beautiful Tamar Lake, a bird sanctuary as well as a reservoir for Bude and Stratton. From there continue into Bradworthy, soon visible on its 600-ft hill. Bradworthy has some attractive Georgian and earlier houses round its wide square and the medieval church stands just off it. Drive past the church on the Holsworthy road and continue through hill pastures as far as Chilsworthy, a direct way which is well signposted, but at the village sign turn right for Pancrasweek, then left at the next T-junction. This brings us in little over a mile to a main road, where we turn left and soon afterwards right for Bridgerule, leaving this road in half a mile for a left turn signposted Derrill and Pyworthy. In the small hamlet of Derrill turn left by a chapel for Pyworthy and steer towards the tall tower of the church, a landmark for this hilltop village. When we reach it we turn right beyond the church for North Tamerton, bearing left out of the village and going forward at the next crossroads and the subsequent junction.

Thereafter follow the signposts to Tamerton, recrossing the Tamar by an old stone bridge into the village, which we drive through with the church on our right and go straight on for two and a half miles through farming countryside interspersed with patches of woodland to reach a T-junction with B3254. Here turn right for Whitstone, just over a mile away, where after passing the turning to the church take the next road to the left and shortly turn right for Titson. We descend steeply through the wooded landscape and after being joined by a lane from the right turn right at a junction signposted Marhamchurch and Stratton. At the next T-junction by a group of farm buildings turn left and keep left again where Widemouth is signposted. Once again turn

D.C.—9

left at a T-junction, this time for Poundstock, and just short of the
large thatched house at Week Orchard turn right where the
signpost shows Poundstock and Widemouth.

A mile along this narrow lane we find the entrance to Penfound
Manor, a fascinating manor-house mentioned in Domesday Book,
parts of it dating back to Saxon times. It is open on Monday and
Friday afternoons from Good Friday to the end of September.
From the manor continue to the main road and cross it to see the
tiny village of Poundstock, an attractive group consisting of
church, guildhall and farm set in woodland. Not only is the
church interesting, with some good wood carving and traces of
frescoes, but the guildhall is a well-preserved fourteenth-century
buttressed building. We can continue past the church to regain
the main road where the way is to the left for Stratton or Bude.

Tour five: Bodmin Moor

No exploration of Cornwall would be complete without a tour
on Bodmin Moor, which has its own distinctive landscapes and
features of interest unseen by those who merely drive swiftly
across it on A30. The tour is planned from Bodmin to Launceston
and back but as it covers only about sixty miles it would not be
too long from the coastal towns, either of the north or south,
within reasonable distance of Bodmin or Launceston. We leave
Bodmin by the Liskeard road (A38) past the museum and market
house decorated by a row of cattle heads, driving above a densely
wooded valley and passing a high wheel-head cross at Carminow
Cross, and soon descend into the beautiful wooded valley of the
river Fowey. This is one of the finest valley roads in Cornwall
and although it is a main road must not be missed. It follows
closely the banks of the winding river for over five miles and near
its end, after we have crossed the Fowey and just beyond a large
quarry, we turn left for St Cleer. This straight minor road goes
over high open country for several miles, looking across to
Caradon Hill, recognized by its mast and rising to over 1,200 ft,
at the farthest south-easterly reach of Bodmin Moor.

Before we arrive at St Cleer we pass King Doniert's Stone on
the right. There are actually parts of two cross shafts, but the
larger is inscribed 'Doniert rogavit pro anima' (Doniert ordered
for his soul). It is believed that Doniert was a King of Cornwall
in the ninth century. Beyond the stones turn right for St Cleer,

where the church is a fine one retaining several Norman features, but beyond the church along a turning to the left there is a splendid example of a holy well and well chapel where the spring still flows. It has six round arches on the three open sides and is entered by a modern wrought iron gate patterned with a cross enclosing quatrefoils. Beside the well stands a simple wheel-head cross.

Continue downhill past the well and at the end of the village turn left for Silva, turning right at the next T-junction, then right again where Trethevy Quoit is signposted, turning right twice more to see this gigantic prehistoric burial chamber in a commanding position on a hilltop. The most convenient way to resume our route is to return to the major road and continue for

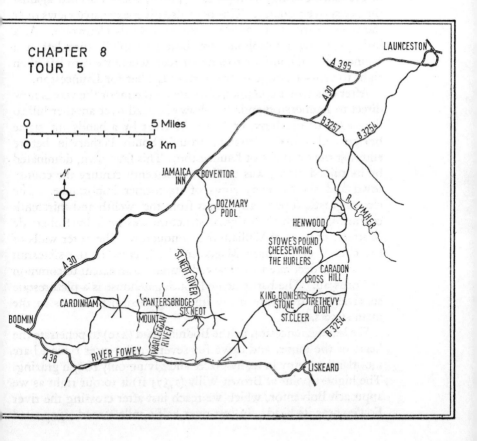

CHAPTER 8
TOUR 5

LAUNCESTON

A 395

A 30

B 3257

B 3254

5 Miles

8 Km

N

JAMAICA INN   BOVENTOR

DOZMARY POOL

R. LYNHER

HENWOOD

STOWE'S POUND
CHEESEWRING
THE HURLERS

CARADON
CROSS HILL

ST. NEOT RIVER

A 30

KING DONIERTS
STONE   TRETHEVY
QUOIT

CARDINHAM   PANTERSBRIDGE
ST. NEOT   ST. CLEER

BODMIN   MOUNT

WARLEGGAN RIVER

B 3254

A 38   RIVER FOWEY

LISKEARD

half a mile until we come to a road signposted on the right for The Hurlers and Launceston. Now we are up on the breezy moor, our road rising to over 1,000 ft and giving extensive vistas in all directions with many old chimneys of mines dotted about the landscape. Soon after passing a simple cross near the highest point a sign indicates on the left the track to The Hurlers, three prehistoric stone circles to which legend has attached the story that they represent a party of men playing the game of hurling on a Sunday who were turned into stone for their impiety.

From the neighbouring hamlet of Cheesewring a track leads up to a natural formation known as the Cheesewring, above which there is a Bronze Age fort known as Stowe's Pound. By turning left for Henwood just beyond the hamlet we can get a better view of the Cheesewring, its top-heavy pile of rocks outlined against the sky above a quarry. This road also gives extensive views over the moor to the right as we continue towards Henwood. At a little green by a telephone box bear left uphill, turn left at a T-junction, and continue to a major road where we turn left, then right to cross a bridge over the river Lynher for Launceston.

After this rather complicated route off the moor the way is now direct to Launceston and we follow the road over another hill to the valley of the Inny, crossing the river by a handsome stone bridge and shortly driving through South Petherwin before entering the outskirts of Launceston. This fine town, dominated by its ruined castle, was until the nineteenth century the county town and shows many signs of its former importance. The circular castle (open daily) dates from the twelfth and thirteenth centuries, though the original structure was built by Robert de Mortain, brother of William the Conqueror. The outer walls of the church of St Mary Magdalene built early in the sixteenth century are decorated with carved granite to an extent uncommon in Cornwall. The battlemented south gatehouse is a picturesque survival and there are many imposing Georgian houses in the main streets.

We leave Launceston by the Bodmin road (A30) to penetrate the heart of the moor, and drive for several miles over typical bare moorland, marshy in many places and giving only rough grazing. The highest point at Brown Willy (1,375 ft) is to our right as we approach Bolventor, which we reach just after crossing the river Fowey near its head. In just over half a mile a road signposted

Liskeard follows the river closely across the moor to its south-eastern boundary. We, however, on this occasion take a road signposted Dozmary Pool starting beside the war memorial opposite the Jamaica inn at Bolventor, one that has only been made up fully in recent years as a through road to the south. It follows the shore of Dozmary Pool on its way across the moor, the shallow lake that has the distinction of being the largest true lake in Cornwall, and the only other striking feature in the bare expanses of coarse grass, supporting hardy cattle and sheep, is the large pyramid of a china clay works. Soon after leaving this behind us we come off the moor into kinder landscapes and shortly turn right at a crossroads for St Neot.

In St Neot we go on past the fine church, noted for the beautiful stained-glass windows containing half the original medieval glass, and the rest well restored. Beyond the church cross the St Neot river and go forward for Mount and Cardinham across a high common for the first mile, dropping down to a well-wooded valley to cross the Warleggan river at Pantersbridge, then up through Mount and over the downs again, maintaining our forward direction until we reach an old cross, where we turn left down a tree-lined road to the village of Cardinham, turning left at the crossroads to pass the church. From here we follow the road through fine woods and gorse-covered commons all the way to the main road, where the way is to the right into Bodmin.

INDEX OF PLACES

Motoring on Regional Byways Series
by Christopher Trent

*To serve as companions and guides to places of natural
beauty and historic interest along unfrequented ways*

NORTH OF LONDON

Byway motoring within a 50-mile radius of the metropolis north
of the Thames.

LAKELAND

Byway motoring in Cumberland, Westmorland and the Furness
district of Lancashire.

MIDLAND ENGLAND

Byway motoring within a 50-mile radius of Birmingham and the
Black Country.

SOUTH OF LONDON

Byway motoring in Surrey, Kent and Sussex.

WEST COUNTRY

Byway motoring in Somerset, Gloucestershire, Herefordshire,
Shropshire, Worcestershire.

BORDER COUNTRY

Byway motoring in Northumberland, Durham and the border
country of Scotland.